P9-DMJ-920

Kitchen Design

for the 21st Century

FRONT
REAR
OVEN
FRONT
REAR
OVEN
FRONT
REAR

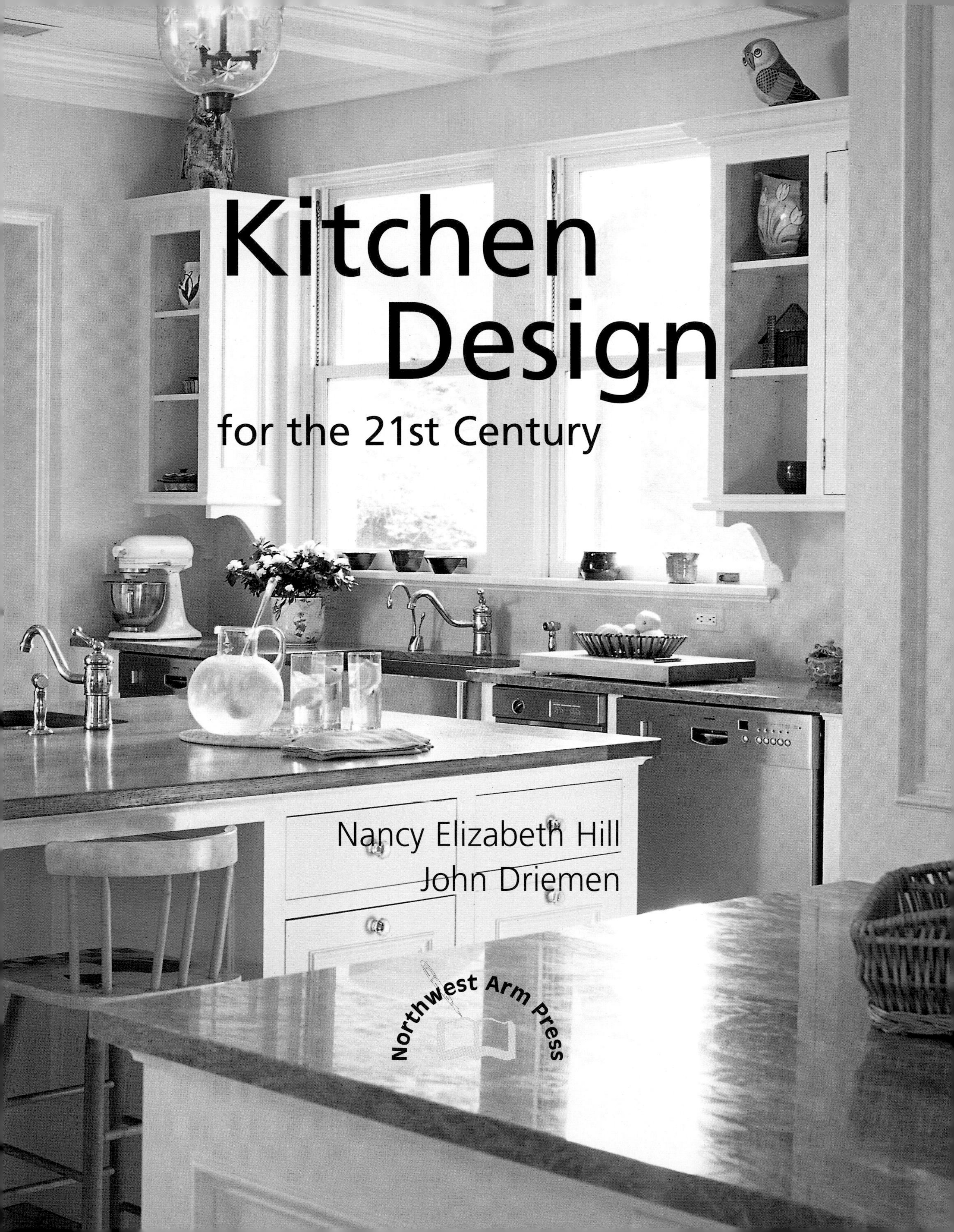
Kitchen
Design
for the 21st Century
Nancy Elizabeth Hill
John Driemen
Northwest Arm Press

Acknowledgments

Nancy Hill and I would like to thank all the homeowners who graciously allowed us into their homes and let us disrupt their lives so that we could get the photographs that appear in this book. Without their generosity and cooperation this book could not have been produced, and we want to add a special thanks to the kitchen designers, builders, and decorators who took the time to talk with us about what they did for these homeowners. We also want to thank North Star Kitchens in Minneapolis, Abruzzo Kitchens in Chicago, and Kitchens by Deane in Stamford, Connecticut for opening up their showrooms to our camera, incurring what I'm sure was a certain inconvenience.

John Driemen would like to thank the staff at the Kroch Library at Cornell University in Ithaca, New York who allowed me to look through Rose Steidl's papers and publications and who granted us permission to publish some of the historical kitchen photographs in their collection. They went out of their way to treat me, a kitchen writer, like a visiting scholar.

Nancy would especially like to thank William and Montgomery. You guys are the best! Florence Hill for your inspiration, patience, and loving care of us all. To Gloria and Aldo, a heartfelt *mille grazie*. Also thanks to Stephen, Robert, Charmin and Doug Hill, and Thomas.

Rick, thanks for being there for the weather, witchiness and all else—still.

Thanks also to Mark and Cathy at Connecticut Photographics, the best damn lab and people out there. Thanks To Kyle Riccoboni, Carolyn Shultz, Sarah Shaw and Tina Armstrong—stylists extraordinaire.

Thanks to Chris Madden and Kristen Ohnmacht, to Ben Horn, Karen Parks, Jackie K., Evelyn, Joe B., Dawn T., Mark F., Chuck Wow, Laurel C., and Elaine S.,Teri G., Fred Allen, Tim Emerson and Dhan. Thanks to the ladies at the bus stop.

Thank you to Cathy at Design within Reach, and Maureen O. and to Curt G. for sharing your friends and your great space in Carmel.

In memory of Bob Sweet and his incredible sense of design, humor and *joie de vivre* and to all those Helen Mooneys and the Minnesota gals out there who love to cook.

Published by Northwest Arm Press, Inc. Halifax, Nova Scotia
Designed and produced by Northwest Arm Press, Inc.

Library and Archives Canada Cataloguing in Publication

Hill, Nancy E. (Nancy Elizabeth) Kitchen Design for the 21st Century
Nancy Elizabeth Hill, John Driemen. -- 2nd ed.

Includes index. ISBN 978-0-9811335-0-8

1. Kitchens--Design and construction. 2. Kitchens--Designs and plans.
3. Kitchens--Planning. I. Driemen, John II. Title.

TH4816.3.K58 H55 2009 747.7'97 C2009-901254-5

10 9 8 7 6 5 4 3 2 1
Second Edition
Printed in China

Introduction

Kitchen design has changed. The ideas behind kitchen design today are very different from those of just ten years ago. So different that we call this book *Kitchen Design for the 21st Century* to set it apart from the ideas of the 1990s. What these 21st century kitchens do and how they do it will determine kitchen design trends for the foreseeable future. Flexibility and adaptability will be the underlying themes that drive homeowners and the designers they hire.

The 21st century kitchen is a work center kitchen. If you aren't familiar with work center kitchens it's probably because you've grown up believing the only way to lay out an efficient kitchen is by following the rules of the kitchen work triangle. This just isn't so, especially with bigger kitchens. Some of the ideas in this book are brand new to this century, if not brand new to you. Some aren't, because they are not new; they were developed almost sixty years ago, but only infrequently applied to kitchen design until recently. They are catching on fast.

In the first part of this book we'll tell you about these old ideas, which are new again. We'll tell you why a work center approach to kitchen design is the right approach for 21st century lifestyles. We'll focus on the centers that make a work center kitchen perform so well. We'll show you why they are the right ideas for larger kitchens and for kitchens that are part of larger, open greatroom spaces.

The second part of the book—the longer part—is a tour through twenty kitchens that demonstrate the ideas we talk about in part 1. We'll be speaking with the designers who put these ideas into practice for people just like you. Some of the homeowners will talk specifically about what they wanted and how they use the kitchens they got. What these designers and homeowners have today represents the latest thinking in work center kitchen design.

But kitchens are more than efficient space plans that make cooking and family activities easier. When we asked the twenty homeowners about what they wanted in their new kitchen, they all said they wanted to smile when they walked into it. That smile, day in and day out, was high on everyone's wish list. If seeing these kitchens makes you smile and if the kitchen you design for yourself as a result of this book makes you smile even more, then Nancy and I have accomplished what we set out to do.

Now let's get started with your new 21st century kitchen.

Contents

VIKING

1

The Design Concept

In the 21st century, kitchens will be designed to fit any lifestyle. There will be specialized work centers based on a new approach to space planning—one developed 60 years ago.

The 21st century kitchen was born at Cornell University in upstate New York in 1947. The ideas for it were developed by Mary Koll Heiner and Rose Steidl at the university's College of Home Economics. Their 1947 research and real-life testing was, as they said at the time, "directed toward integrating work centers in the kitchen to simplify the work performed there and to economize the use of the worker's [the cook's] body." They saw a functional kitchen as one that fit both the worker and the work to be done. They learned, through testing various kitchen layouts, that working in the kitchen could be made easier by the sensible arrangement of what they called "work centers." More testing showed that well-organized storage located at or near these work centers made them work even better. This was the beginning of what is now called "work center kitchen design."

So why look back; why this kitchen history? The answer is easy. What's old is new again. Work centers, the direct descendants of Heiner and Steidl's research, are what make the 21st century kitchen so versatile, so efficient and so adaptable to the demands we make on it. Knowing why and how work centers worked sixty years ago will help you understand why they will work for you today. We promise to keep this short, and there won't be a test.

Three Questions

Three questions motivated Heiner and Steidl in 1947: How can you arrange your kitchen to make your work easier? What are the things your family wants to do most in the kitchen? Do you want your kitchen to be a living kitchen—a room that is the shared activity center of the home? Sound familiar? Perhaps you've been asking yourself these same questions as you think about remodeling that old kitchen of yours. They are the basis of any wish list, the first step toward a new kitchen.

Understanding the principles of Work Center design

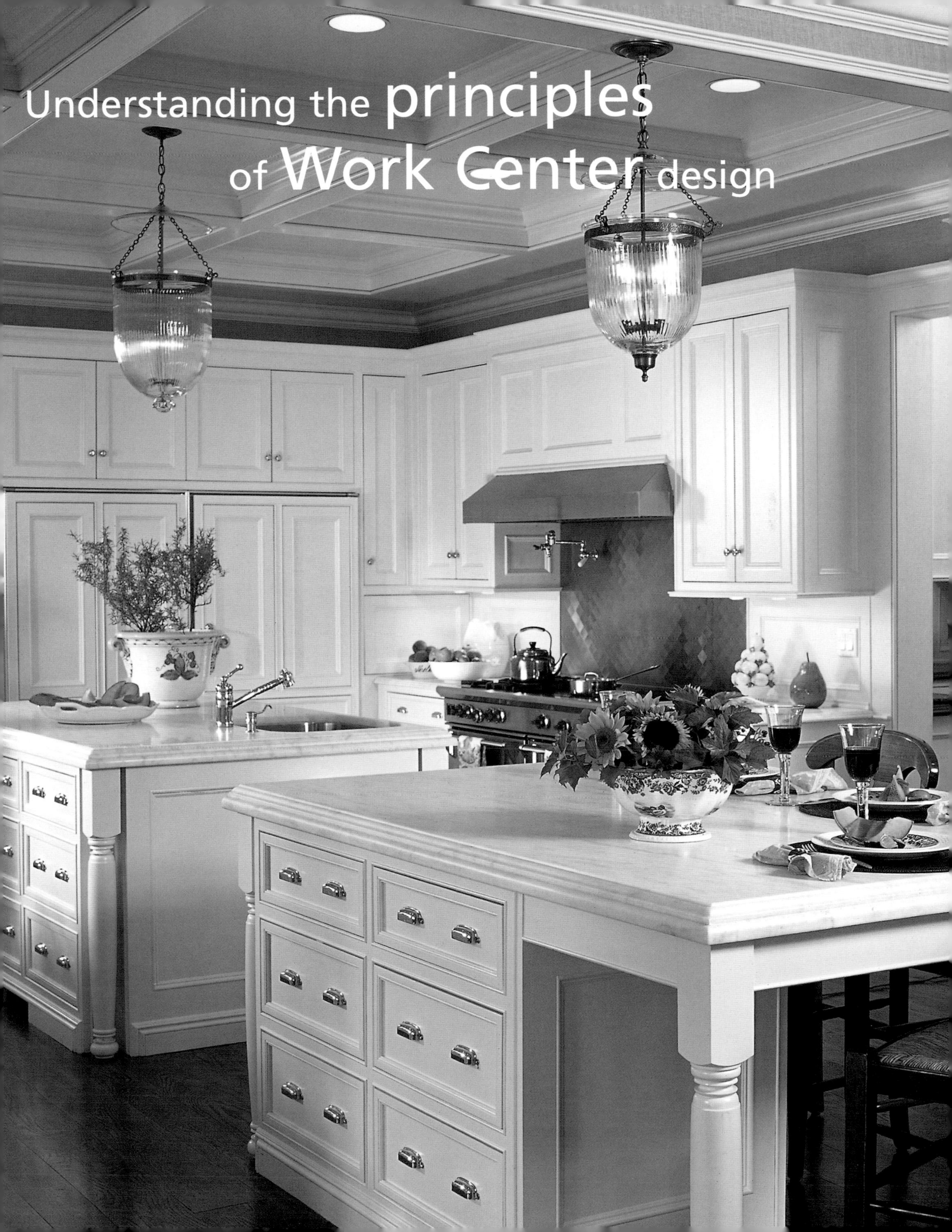

Elements that make a Work Center kitchen work

The Food Storage Center localizes this function in a single one part of the kitchen A large refrigerator is positioned next to a walk-in pantry. The island has places to set-down grocery bags close to where things will be put away.

A Snack Center for the kids keeps them out of the cook's way. The microwave is near the freezer for quick and easy access to frozen foods. Putting it on this side of the kitchen makes it convenient for the kids to use, and close to the counter where they eat. A water cooler makes this snack center even more versatile.

A Casual Eating Area for the kids. This multi-use island gives them a place to eat and do homework. A divider separates their side of the island from the food preparation counter where their parents work.

The Cooking Center has a six burner commercial style cooktop with a cold water spigot to fill big pots on the spot. There is plenty of counter space on both sides of the cooktop, and the cook has close access to a butcherblock plating counter.

The Baking Center includes a marble countertop—the ideal material for rolling out pastry. The counter is lowered for less muscle strain and is close to both the ovens and and the prep sink. Customized drawers below the counter store supplies and utensils, much the same way they were stored in Hoosier cabinets 60 years ago,

The Fresh Food Prep Center, anchored by a prep sink, has plenty of work counter space for chopping foods and getting them ready for cooking. A pair of refrigerator drawers in base cabinets next to the sink stores fresh produce close to where it will be washed.

A high counter at the end of the island, gives both cooks a place where they can stand and browse through recipes.

The Clean-up Center is where the everyday dishes are stored in cabinets next to the kitchen's main dishwasher. Since it's next to the table where the family eats. these dishes are close to where they will be used.

Heiner and Steidl sought the answers through a series of tests using volunteers preparing typical meals. Results showed that kitchen tasks from preparation through cleanup were most efficiently handled by five task-specific work centers, which they ranked according to how often each was used. The sink center came in first since it was used for both food preparation and cleanup. Next came the range center. If you had a "two-piece range," which is what the primitive cooktops and wall ovens of the time were called, this became two centers: the oven center and the surface cooking center. Third was the mix center. Here was where you mixed, prepared, and assembled ingredients for meals; this included baking. The mix center took its cue from the Hoosier cabinet, the must-have accessory of its day. The Hoosier was the ultimate kitchen organizer. Packed into a single free-standing cabinet were bins used to store flour, sugar, and other staples. The bins were mounted above an enameled work surface. Spouts on the bins let the flour and sugar pour straight into bowls. Below the work surface was a drawer for utensils and, below that, cabinet space for storing pots, pans, pie plates, and bowls.

The refrigerator center and the china center tied for fourth. China centers provided storage for the dishes, silverware, and glasses used at the table. Remember, this was 1947, a time when dining rooms were used every day. Storing plates and serving pieces near the dining room table made sense.

First-Use Storage

Heiner and Steidl's research led to the principle of storing items close to where they are first used. Since the sink was the most important work center, they suggested that utensils needed for food preparation at the sink be stored near it. They called this area "sink first-use storage." In recommending what sort of utensils should be stored here and at other storage points in the kitchen, they gave preference to what was needed for the different tasks of food preparation at each work center: knives near where things were chopped, frying pans closer to the range, that sort of thing.

Watching the volunteer cooks work in the different test-kitchen layouts, Heiner and Steidl saw that most meals demanded moving regularly between the sink and range centers. Layouts that worked best had the sink and range positioned side by side or at right angles to each other. Either way, the cook could see what was cooking on the range from her position at the sink by just turning her head. Walking away from the sink wasn't necessary.

The location of the mix center depended on how the cook liked to work. One layout put it next to the sink; others placed it in between the sink and the range on the same wall, what we would call a galley kitchen today. The volunteer cooks found that they made more trips between the mix center and the sink than between the mix center and the range or between the mix center and the refrigerator.

Five or more appliances do not fit easily into small triangular spaces.

Adding a Second Sink

None of these ideas are far removed from what we recognize today as the basics of good space planning for smaller kitchens. If Steidl's inquiries had stopped here, she would not have earned her place as the mother of modern kitchen design. But they didn't. In the mid 1950s, she tested an idea that would change how kitchens looked and worked. Steidl believed that for maximum efficiency, kitchens needed more than one sink. More tests with volunteer cooks proved this and led to suggested locations for the second sink.

These tests showed that a second sink was most useful in food preparation because it gave cooks a second water source—a place to clean and drain food and wash their hands. Test subjects found that the second sink tended to define the role of the primary sink as the

Two popular work centers in a 21st century kitchen are the snack center for kids, top, and a planning center for the parents, above. This snack center has a small wine cooler used to hold milk and juice. Both centers would be hard to fit into a work triangle kitchen.

Elements of the Work Triangle kitchen

The Work Triangle hasn't changed much in 65 years; what has changed is how we live

KITCHEN WORK TRIANGLE. CIRCA 1940

KITCHEN WORK TRIANGLE. CIRCA 2009

The basic work triangle kitchen was developed in the 1930s. Only three appliances counted: the sink, range and refrigerator. Back then, of course, only three appliances were available. Placing them in a triangular floor plan centralized food preparation and cooking tasks within the triangle.

The 1940s era kitchen is a cul-de-sac. No one can walk through the kitchen to hinder the cook working at her tasks. In the 2003 version, traffic has to move through the triangle to get to other places in the house, potentially disrupting kitchen efficiency.

Note the different counter heights in the 1940s kitchen—an idea that's just now being rediscovered. During the intervening years cabinet manufactures kept counter heights at a standard 36 inches, making the mass production of base cabinets more profitable.

cleanup center. The volunteers preferred a second sink near the range but couldn't see its usefulness when placed near the refrigerator. Steidl concluded that a second sink close to the range significantly improved the way a kitchen functioned—something we'd all agree with today. Steidl published her findings about second sinks in 1957 and 1961. Few people took any notice.

Mix centers, then and now. The Hoosier cabinet, top, with its convenient, task-specific storage was the prototype for today's baking center, above.

Work Triangles

The reason why people didn't notice was because of the kitchen work triangle—the other approach to kitchen design. Even though Heiner and Steidl showed that the typical early 1950s housewife appreciated those five work centers; and that Steidl independently proved the value of two sinks, the work triangle, with its single sink, became the standard for kitchen design. It remained so for forty years.

The thinking—actually the geometry—behind the work triangle goes something like this: Every kitchen has a range, a refrigerator, and a sink—just like Steidl's research kitchens at Cornell. These appliances are placed so that they form the points of a triangle. The legs of this triangle are the paths walked between the range, sink, and refrigerator during meal preparation. Efficiency in a work triangle kitchen is measured by the number of steps taken as you move about the triangle when preparing and cooking a meal. The fewer, the better.

The National Kitchen & Bath Association (NKBA), a proponent of kitchen work triangles and over the years the developer of the space-planning standards based on a triangular positioning of appliances, suggests that the maximum total distance of the triangle, the sum of the leg lengths, not exceed 26 feet. The group also says that no leg should be greater than 9 feet nor less than 4 feet. But kitchens are getting bigger, much bigger. Distances between cooking appliances, sinks, refrigerators—big kitchens often duplicate these appliances—and the other functional components in a large kitchen can easily exceed 9 feet. At what point does the triangle become so big that the kitchen is no longer an efficient place to work?

Problems with Work Triangles

Proponents of work triangle design don't have a good answer. This leads to some lively debates with designers who support work center space planning. The issues are not black and white; there is some common ground. The range in a work triangle kitchen does the same thing that it does in a work center kitchen. Both design approaches call this part of the kitchen the cooking center. The same thing with the sink—remember that a basic work triangle kitchen only has one—which in both systems is called the cleanup center.

Similarities stop here. In a work triangle kitchen, the refrigerator is considered a center—both the place for food storage and the anchor appliance for that part of the kitchen where food is prepared before it's cooked. By contrast, in a work center kitchen there is a specific area for food preparation, usually anchored by a second sink. In today's bigger kitchens, refrigerators are often placed along the kitchen perimeter and are part of a storage wall, flanked by full-height cabinets, perhaps one of them a pantry. Taken together, this wall becomes the primary storage center in a work center kitchen.

Islands are catalysts that make work center kitchens perform at their best.

What about that second sink that Steidl determined in 1957 to be so important to the efficiency of any kitchen? L-shaped and U-shaped kitchen layouts that create neat work triangles have no obvious place for it.

This isn't to say that the work triangle wasn't or isn't an efficient way to space-plan kitchens. It worked fine, as far as it went. Arranging the sink, range and refrigerator in an L-shape or U-shape layout, forming a proper triangle, automatically created plenty of storage in the form of long runs of base cabinets with matching wall cabinets above. In these popular triangular layouts there was no need for walk-in pantries and Hoosiers. What they did was to create an expanding market for kitchen cabinet manufactures and a standardization of cabinets into stock sizes. Kitchen plans and counter lengths reflected the fact that base cabinets ranged from 12 to 48 inches in 3-inch increments. Everyone became comfortable with L-shape and U-shape layouts into which stock cabinet sizes fitted nicely.

New Technologies

Then technology took a hand in kitchen design, starting with the microwave. When this originally bulky appliance shrank to where it could mount in a cabinet instead of having to sit on a counter or kitchen cart, it caught on as a must-have appliance. Designers, supported by manufacturers, quickly suggested that the best place for it was above the range—part of the cooking center. Over time, people began to see the microwave as a stand-alone appliance. They thought it should be closer to a freezer where it could be used to defrost meats or quickly cook prepared, frozen meals. Where was this place in a work triangle?

As families began to do everything in a hurry, the microwave came into its own as the cooking appliance that could best meet the "right now"attitude of kids, especially as every night sit-down family meals were little more than a memory. This led to the idea of the snack center. Where do you put this in a triangular layout?

What about a planning center? No one thought of this sixty years ago. Then, searching for recipes, writing shopping lists, or paying bills were done at a kitchen table or at a counter. Today, many people want a computer station in the kitchen so they can go online to shop. They want a desk for organizing all the paperwork that's part of being married with children. It has to fit somewhere, but where?

Planning centers, snack centers, food prep centers, and storage centers are what make 21st century kitchens work. So why did it take almost fifty years for work centers to catch on? One reason is that for

The evolution of islands

Islands started out as small tables that could be moved into the center of the kitchen where they could be used as food preparations areas allowing you to work sitting down

Today islands have evolved into important functional elements of the work center kitchen design. They provide locations for the second sink, like this island, and a specialized appliance—the wine cooler. There's also ample space for food preparation and eating. Note that the counter overhangs the island to create a knee space for the stools.

most of these years, kitchens were smaller and often separate rooms closed off by doors. There wasn't enough space for all these work centers, nor had the new appliances and convenience gadgets that required this additional space or at least a different approach to space planning to make them fit, been invented yet.

The kitchen work triangle was developed when there were only three appliances: the range—which included an oven below the surface cooking units—the refrigerator, and the sink. The dishwasher was just becoming popular. There were no refrigerator drawers, ice makers, or wine coolers; no dishwasher drawers, microwaves, or convection ovens. Now there are. Slavishly trying to fit five or six appliances, plus a second sink, into a layout formula originally designed for three can lead to frustration during the planning stage, and design mistakes that will come back to bite you when the project is done.

Lifestyle Changes

Something else that held back implementation of work center design principles was a more traditional lifestyle that the baby boomers grew up in. Fathers worked; mothers stayed at home with the kids. Meals were eaten in the dining room; there were only four channels on the TV, and no video games. Computers hadn't been invented. Well, those days are gone. We are casual in everything we do; family members are always on the go, each needing to get things done and a place to do them.

In this on-the-go lifestyle, the kitchen is a grand central station for family activities of all kinds. This is

Pantries are another old idea coming back into vogue. The specialized storage spaces in the 1940s-era pantry, top, may surprise those who think this kind of specialization is brand new. Also back are butler's pantries, left. Once a sign of affluence in large homes with servants, today's version combines efficient storage with the additional counter space so useful when you entertain.

where the kids do their homework during the week, where you have friends over for supper on Saturday, and where you watch football on Sunday. If you need a family meeting, this is where it happens.

Cooking is no longer just a woman's work. Men cook—and like to. Kids cook, too. If you're having a party, several people could be cooking at once. In fact, having space for more than one cook is high on many wish lists. This means that space has to be found so that two people don't continually bump into each other. This space isn't usually inside the confines of a work triangle.

The Walls Come Down

Both the original work triangle and Steidl's early work center kitchens envisioned a kitchen enclosed by four walls, with a door leading to a dining room and maybe a door leading to the outside. That's the way kitchens looked in the 1940s and 1950s, and these competing design approaches set out to make the best of the contemporary conditions.

Today, there are no partition walls. Kitchens are part of open living areas that include a place for casual eating and a family room. Often, there will be a home entertainment center focusing on a wide-screen TV. The dining room is pretty much a thing of the past. If used at all, it's only at the holidays: Thanksgiving, Christmas, or Passover.

Open plan kitchens, with their adjacent family rooms, great rooms, or casual living spaces led to the use of kitchen islands. Islands do important things. They add useful counter space to the kitchen and provide an almost automatic location for a second sink, or cooktop closer to a sink—an arrangement of centers that reflects Steidl's idea that the cook shouldn't have to walk away from the sink in order to check on what's on the stove. Islands add storage space, cut down the walking distances between work centers, and establish traffic patterns that direct people easily through the kitchen and out of the cook's way.

Large islands function like big tables, providing room to eat or to put food out for buffet parties. They have lots of space for younger kids to do crafts or play games. For older ones, it's an after-dinner homework area—mom or dad, finishing cleanup chores, close by to answer questions. Islands are also natural room dividers. In open plans they are shared elements between rooms, with specialized storage on both sides. They are also a shared design element.

This brings us to the middle of the first decade of the 21st century and today's work center kitchen, the direct descendent of the work done by Steidl and Heiner. But first one more brief look back. A 1948 pamphlet written by Heiner, called *Functional Kitchen Storage,* has the following three suggestions on its first page: Build the cabinets to fit the woman. Build the shelves to fit the supplies. Build the kitchen to fit the family. Forgetting the politically incorrect language of the time, everyone planning a new kitchen today should keep these suggestions in mind. Helping you do that is what the next chapter is all about.

Build the cabinets to fit the cook.

Build the shelves for what you store.

Build the kitchen to fit the family.

2

Elements of Design

In the 21st century kitchen, work centers focusing on storage, lifestyle, personal style, and convenience for the kids will be just as important as the traditional cooking and cleanup centers.

We'll start by looking at the work centers that go into a 21st century kitchen: We'll see what they do, why they are important, and where they should go in your kitchen. Then we'll examine hidden elements of design that make 21st century kitchens so adaptable to today's lifestyle.

First the work centers.

How many work centers you want or need depends on how you use your kitchen, whether you have a family, and how old your children are. Ask yourself this, too: Do two people cook regularly? Is the kitchen a focal point for parties? How does it relate to the rooms around it? One thing is for sure, you'll want more than the five centers Steidl tested at Cornell sixty years ago. Because you'll certainly want at least two sinks—as Steidl suggested, the sink center is a good place to begin our kitchen tour.

Sink Centers

Their importance today is the same as it was in the 1940s. The primary sink, almost always the larger one, is used most for cleanup. The dishwasher goes next to it; together they form the cleanup center. The second sink is for food preparation: washing vegetables, filling cooking pots, a quick hands' wash, that sort of thing. The second sink should be located as close to the surface cooking units as possible. In this position, with plenty of countertop around it, it becomes the key element of your kitchen's food preparation center. To get the most out of a two-sink kitchen, plan the layout so the second sink anchors that food preparation area, and locate the sinks as far apart from each other as is practicable.

Cooking Centers

In a 21st century kitchen there can be one, or as many as three or four, cooking centers in task-specific locations. Commercial-style gas ranges are popular with people who like to cook. They provide six or eight burners, sometimes a grill and griddle combination, and one or two ovens. If this is what you want, and all you want, your kitchen will have a single cooking center. If you don't want a commercial-style range, or any range, the most common pairing is a cooktop and two wall ovens You can get the same high-power burners in a cooktop as you can with a commercial-style range.

Splitting your cooking appliances means that surface cooking can be done with gas, while baking and roasting are done in electric ovens. Serious bakers, who prefer the heat from an electric oven, are likely to want this. A wall oven often anchors a baking center that includes specialized storage, a marble counter to roll out dough and setdown space where just-baked items can cool down.

Ranges generally go against a wall because in this location it's easier to install the proper ventilation to exhaust heat, moisture and cooking odors. Grottoes that visually frame a commercial range against the rest of the kitchen are popular today. The grotto also hides the ventilation hood, which in a more traditional-looking kitchen, most people do not want to see. If you prefer a cooktop, efficient downdraft ventilation systems let you install the cooktop in an island and get the same exhaust power as from an overhead vent hood.

There are times when a task-specific cooking appliance—such as a gas wok burner or separate

Understanding the elements of Work Center design

electric steamer—solves a specific cooking problem. These specialized appliances, with their downdraft ventilation if required, are often on counters in other parts of the kitchen, away from the range or cooktop where they create another cooking center.

Food Preparation Centers

Picking the right location for the food preparation center, with its prep sink, is your first and most important space-planning task. Steidl's real-life testing showed that the preparation center should be close to the surface cooking area—steps away, perhaps right next to it. Chris Donner, a kitchen designer from Connecticut who designed one of the kitchens you'll see later on in this book, has a name for the area between these two centers. She calls it "the trench." This is where at least one cook spends most of his or her time, moving back and forth in it. Make sure the trench in your kitchen is out of the main traffic path that people take through the kitchen.

Refrigeration

In a 21st century kitchen, refrigeration won't always be in one location. It's no longer a point on a triangle. Large capacity refrigerators and freezers go where they are needed, sometimes split up and put at different ends of the kitchen. Refrigerators and freezers work in conjunction with other work centers rather than form their own center. If you want only one refrigerator-freezer combination, put it outside the trench but easily accessible to where you cook and also where kids can get to it from another room without walking through the trench. That way workflow won't be interrupted by their comings and goings. Refrigerator drawers, beverage coolers, and ice makers mean that task-specific cooling can go exactly where it's needed. A refrigerator drawer, for example, near the prep sink is the right place to store fresh produce that will need to be washed. A freezer drawer near the microwave is the right spot for quick-cook frozen snack foods.

Planning Centers

We talked a bit about planning centers in Chapter 1—a work center never considered by either the early work triangle advocates or by Steidl and her Cornell colleagues. A well-thought-out planning center is the heart of the kitchen when it's not being used for cooking. A planning center belongs on the kitchen's perimeter; you should be able to reach it without walking through the kitchen.

The basic components are a desk area with an electrical outlet and a phone jack in the wall behind the desk, and a comfortable chair. The desk should be big enough for a computer screen or at least a laptop. Make sure that it has a shallow drawer for odds and ends and a deep one that can be used for filing. Your planning center can be a secondary home office, a place for

paying bills, organizing school events for the kids, or just a convenient place to go online when you need to check an airfare or make a bid on eBay.

Snack Centers

Another way to direct the kids away from the trench is to give them a snack center. Like refrigeration, snack centers belong on the kitchen perimeter. Well-equipped ones have a refrigerator drawer or an under-counter beverage cooler—they keep milk and juice just as cold and fresh as they keep beer and wine. The far side of a big island is a good location. So is a place in your kitchen that's close to a door leading outside. Another option is to put it close to where the kids watch TV or play videos. If your kids use a microwave to heat frozen snack foods, combining a microwave with a remote freezer drawer will give them what they need. Mounting a microwave used mostly by kids at their shoulder height is good safety feature.

Wetbars

Wetbars are small service areas away from the main kitchen area. They always include a small sink—the water source is what gives them their name—and are often accompanied by an ice maker. Sometimes a small under-counter refrigerator, a refrigerator drawer, or a wine cooler is included. In full service wetbars, you'll find a dishwasher.

Storage at the wetbar is usually customized for glassware and party supplies, with enough counter space to mix drinks and assemble hors d'oeuvres. For smaller gatherings, like a Sunday football afternoon with drinks, dry munchies, and popcorn, a wetbar can do everything the kitchen can and localize the mess.

While well-planned and well-positioned work centers give you a kitchen capable of meeting changing family and social needs, other important considerations affect both how it functions and how it looks. We call these the "hidden" elements of design, hidden because they are less noticeable and less likely to be written about. If noticed at all, it's because these elements aren't there. Causing you say to yourself, "Hey, something's missing here."

The rest of this chapter looks at these hidden elements: lighting, how to use color to unify a large open space that includes the kitchen and adjacent living areas, interesting new small appliances, and showing off your personality with collectibles. But we'll start with a design element that is hidden, in the truest sense of the word: good storage.

The number of **work centers** you have depends on how you use your **kitchen.**

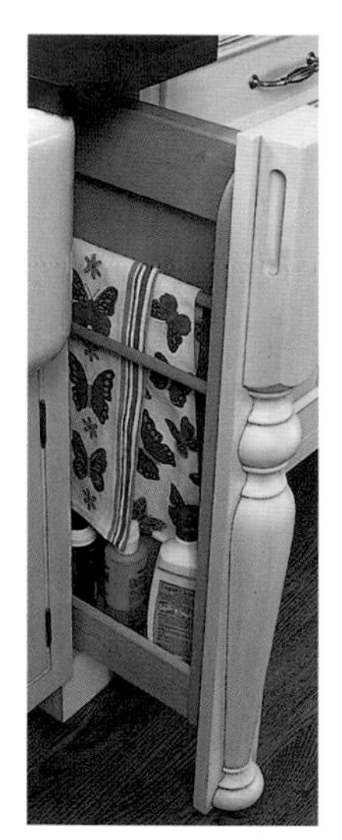

A wide array of customized storage options is available today—all aimed at keeping things where you need them. Deep drawers can be customized to hold pots or just their lids. Shallow drawers come with every kind of insert you can think of for storing silverware, kitchen knives, and utensils.

Mechanical inserts find space in formerly useless corner cabinets. Racks under cooktops hold large pots that seldom fit elsewhere, and 6-inch wide pull-outs can hold everything from spices to dish towels.

Storing the stuff where you use it first

Having enough storage won't be a problem in the 21st century kitchen. Bigger kitchens will automatically provide the space you need. More important is how storage can be organized so you won't be running all over to find what you need.

Which brings us back to the Heiner and Steidl's principle of storage based on the point of first use. Simply put, this means that pots and pans should be stored near the surface cooking units, knives and measuring cups near the food prep areas, and dishes close to where you plate your meals. For real efficiency, dish and glassware storage should also be close to a dishwasher. Keep snack foods close to where you want your kids to eat them—or hope they will eat them. If there are two cooks, don't hesitate to double up on key items—two sets of knives if there are two prep areas, or a prep area and a baking center.

Think through your storage requirements before you buy the cabinets. Make a list of what you need to put away and decide where you want to put it.

Efficient storage isn't limited to what's kept behind closed doors. The glass jars, top, holding all sorts of staples are eye-catchers. When placed near a prep counter, their contents are conveniently available when needed as ingredients.

More often, special storage solutions are built into places designed to accommodate them. Movable drawer pegs, above, can be arranged to hold different dish sizes, while appliances garages, right, are perfect toasters, mixers and the like.

Big pantries are returning to kitchens now that kitchens are large enough to have them. There are two kinds:

Butler's pantries are open, separate rooms off the kitchen, usually with counters for food preparation or serving buffets. Sometimes they have a sink, dishwasher, refrigerator, or a warming drawer. Bulter's pantries often connect the kitchen to an eating area or dining room.

Walk-in pantries are like walk-in closets. They have customized shelf storage, though seldom any appliances, and can always be closed off by a door.

Storing the stuff In pantries

In the 21st century, storage of staples and other non-perishables will be centralized in pantries—a return to an idea popular until the 1950s, before they gave way to long cabinet runs. Pantries are back in fashion because they hold a lot, are easy to organize, and because there is a trend away from using wall cabinets—and the stuff has got to go somewhere. A basic pantry is like a small closet with adjustable shelves, often built-in on one side of the refrigerator.

Pullout pantries—full-height, base cabinet height or some height in between—are options all cabinet manufacturers offer. Their shelf arrangements can be customized to maximize the space behind the door and make the stored items easy to see and reach from both sides of the open pantry.

Putting Things Away

- Store cooking utensils and dishes close to where you first use them.
- If you are left-handed, store your most used utensils where you reach for them with your left hand.
- Heavy items in wall cabinets should be no higher than your shoulders; in base cabinets, no lower than your knees.
- Heavy cooking pots are best stored in drawers directly under the cooktop. If you cook on a range, keep the pots in drawers or on shelves right next to it.
- High shelves in wall cabinets or pantries are the right places for seasonal items.
- Put a refrigerator drawer near a sink to store produce that has to be washed.

Unconventional displays create spectacular effects. The collection of antique storage tubs, above, sits on glass shelves hung from a pipe, itself suspended from the ceiling.

Personalize your kitchen. You're in your kitchen a lot, so you might as well have things around you that you enjoy: a tea cup collection, travel souvenirs, antique pots, anything that expresses your personality; it doesn't matter. Glass door cabinets are a great place to display these items that show off your personality.

These displays should not, however, take away space needed to store things used regularly. Creating nice display spaces is an important part of a good storage plan. That's why you should consider it together with other storage questions.

Cabinet manufacturers sell wall units that make displaying things easy. These have full glass doors and three or more shelves (sometimes glass themselves) to show off your collectibles. Often, the cabinet roof can accommodate a "puck light" for illuminating displayed items. If you want to combine storage with display—a polite way of saying that you may not want to worry about seeing perfectly styled stacks of plates and soup bowls behind glass doors—you can pick a cabinet door that is solid on the lower two-thirds and glass on top.

Showing Off Your Stuff

- Make a display cabinet a visual focal point in your kitchen.
- Suspended cabinets over a peninsula that's used as a room divider provide good places for collectibles because you can see them from two different rooms.
- If collectibles, like cups or china, are used regularly, plan display storage close to where you like to use them.

Let your kitchen show off your personality

Here is a sampling of appliances that goes beyond cooktops and ranges. These task-specific appliances make it possible to have more than one cooking center.

A dual-fuel cooktop and prep sink, right, by designer Troy Adams are recessed into an island.

The energy-efficient side-by-side refrigerator opposite, right, has five temperature zones for customized storage and for blending food and wine storage in one appliance.

The cook sink, opposite page, top right, fills and drains like any other sink but it also cooks. Use it for boiling pasta, for steaming, or to slow-cook soups and stews.

The teppanyaki grill, right, brings Japanese-style grilling to the home kitchen. Two heat zones let you sear meat and fish in the front while keeping vegetables warm in the back.

Refrigerator drawers, opposite page, bottom, are perfect for any small space or to create a snack center. The drawers are deep enough to hold liter bottles of milk and soda.

Appliances your mother never dreamed of

The microwave-in-a-drawer can be installed under the counter or even below a wall oven. Easy to use for left-handers, it features a control lock for child safety.

Welcome to 21st century kitchen technology. It has come a long way in a few years, pushed along by all of us who like to cook.

Most of the really neat stuff is for cooking—not fancy ranges or cooktops, but small, counter-mounted appliances for specialized cooking tasks you might not want to do on a range or cooktop. Refrigerator and freezer drawers let you store fresh produce at the preparation center: juice, milk, and soda at the snack center, and frozen meals near the microwave.

For cleanup chores there are dishwasher drawers. Smaller than traditional dishwashers, they can be put right where you need them: close to the range to wash pots, close to the prep sink to wash mixing bowls and utensils or at the snack center to take care of the kids' dirty dishes.

Where to Put Them

- Steamers, cook sinks and deepfryers can be mounted in any counter. Plan a second, smaller cooking center around them.
- Wok burners and similar cooking appliances should be close to the cooktop or range so they can be vented by a single hood. If located elsewhere, they will need separate venting.
- Refrigerator drawers are best placed near your food preparation center or, if used to keep cold soda for the kids, near the snack center.
- A freezer drawer is usually paired with a refrigerator drawer. Since both drawers will probably be near the prep center, plan to locate your microwave close by and use the freezer drawer to store heat-and-eat convenience meals.
- A dishwasher drawer makes sense near a range or cooktop where it can be used to wash small loads of pots, pans and cooking utensils. Another good place is at the wet bar, where it can handle party glasses and snack plates.

Color draws the eye to what you want people to see. The progression of color from red to yellow, above, moves the eye from the kitchen to a scaled-down eating and work area for small children. Alternatively, the bright red cooking center, below, immediately catches the eye and announces that this is the most important part of this kitchen.

Color is the best tool to integrate a kitchen into the rooms around it. Color makes all rooms warm and inviting and it helps create balance. While paint is the best and fastest way to add color, fabrics also play a part.

For big open-plan spaces, choosing one color for all of the walls will give you the unity you want. Painting large areas in various colors can be jarring to the eyes. There are exceptions. In some big, open-plan spaces, some people like the kitchen to loudly proclaim itself as "The Kitchen." Within a kitchen, contrasting colors or finishes between the cabinets and an island can add both visual impact and visual separation.

The best way to define space and the activities planned for them is with furniture. Think of an island with several bar stools around it as a furniture grouping. Rugs do the same thing. A rug near a lesser-used work center along the edges of the kitchen—a planning center or wetbar center—makes a nice design statement and sets that center off from others in the kitchen. But a rug in the kitchen trench area isn't a good idea. It's too easy to trip over and very likely to get dirty.

Color and texture will unify the open rooms that radiate around the kitchen

The Coloring Book

- Using the same fabric or color scheme in the kitchen and the rooms around it will unify the space.
- If you want white cabinets, think about putting them against a colored wall to create eye-catching interest.
- Painting a small room next to the kitchen a different color will define that room as having a different use.
- Color is subjective. Forget about the old saw that light colors make small rooms seem larger while darker ones hem it in. If a bright color will make you smile, use it.

Green is the new color for today's kitchen design

Green kitchen design has moved beyond the recycling center. In the 21st century green design will be about choosing materials for your kitchen that are both environmentally friendly and renewable: materials like bamboo for veneers, cork for floors and cement for work counters —and recycled products. It will mean materials that are formaldehyde- and PVC-free.

The kitchen shown here is a demonstration from Crystal Cabinetry of what can be done with green products. Cabinet doors are both solid and veneer bamboo in light and dark finishes. The entire floor is cork. The butcher block board at the sink was reclaimed from a lumber yard and the wood beam supporting one end of the island began life as part of a barn. The backsplash is a quarter-inch-thick composite made from 50% postconsumer recycled products.

Going Green

- Buy wood products that are FSC Certified. Certification tells you that the wood has come from a properly managed forest.
- Choose contractors who use adhesives and finishes whose chemical bases will not pollute the atmosphere.
- Ask your kitchen designer or cabinet maker if they have access to and are willing to use recycled materials.
- Shop online for salvaged wood or other recycled products if you cannot find them locally.

Linoleum is the original green flooring product. Developed in the early years of the 20th century from natural materials and linseed oil, it was the flooring of choice until it vanished in the 1970s. Now it's back. The sample squares above are Marmoleum, a modern but still green version of this venerable flooring product.

Green kitchens look like any other kitchen. It's the materials that make the difference. Bamboo for both flooring and cabinets is becoming popular because it is renewable. And counters made from recycled materials are indistinguishable from those that are not.

The first step in green living is to rethink your kitchen with an eco-friendly design

Green living is taking center stage. The design demands for today's kitchens offer opportunities to go green at every turn.

A green kitchen works like any other. The difference is in the materials used: countertops, cabinet fronts and flooring; and in the choice of energy-efficient appliances.

Here's some of what "going green" really means:

Start with energy efficiency—take it beyond local code requirements. Using less electricity and gas or propane makes sense and cents. Think conservation when it comes to a resource we take for granted—water. Pay attention to indoor air quality. We are what we eat and what we breathe. Proper ventilation contributes to your family's good health.

A kid's zone in the kitchen, right, allows a small child to play with favorite toys while a parent cooks and yet be out of the high traffic area of the kitchen. When the child grows up, the cabinets used for the kid's zone can be "recycled" by putting them to use for another purpose.

Solid surface countertops, above, are going green. Once primarily made from plastic-based polymers, you can now find ones made with up to 75% recycled materials. These sustainable counters are beautiful to the eye and perfect for the environment.

Bamboo is a new material of choice in green kitchen design, not only for kitchen cabinets, right, but also for durable flooring and counters. Finishing options allow for interesting color and texture variations.

Green kitchen design finds every inch of valuable space—even formerly forgotten corners. These cleverly stacked drawers, lower right, also made from bamboo, turn a wasted corner into usable drawer storage for small cooking utensils or extra silverware.

Ingredients for Green Kitchens

- Look for cabinets that do not use formaldehyde binders in the manufacturing process. Searching online for green cabinetmakers is a great way to start.
- Buy ENERGY STAR appliances that lower energy costs substantially. With new stringent rules from EPA, these appliances use less water and offer better protection again noise pollution.
- Think about countertops made with a high recycled content. Alternatives are concrete, engineered stone composites and some laminates.
- Seek out stainless steel sinks made from 100% recycled steel. Choose low-flow faucets certified as Water Sense.
- For flooring shop for local lumber from sustainable sources or look for recycled wood. Other green flooring choices include real linoleum, cork and tile made from recycled materials.

3

Family Kitchens

The kitchen is the heart of the home; it has always been so. In the 21st century, kitchens will expand and become the welcoming focal point of family life and a family-oriented lifestyle.

Raising Arizona

In 1936, kitchens were small; they were shut away behind closed doors, and if you had the means, your hired cook was the only person who used it. Not a setup for modern family living. In Tucson, Arizona, however, these older houses had historical significance and architectural features dating from what locals call the Arizona territorial period. Keeping these features and the charm that came with them was, and still is, important when planning a remodeling in Tucson.

This Tucson house fits that bill. The owners were still coping with the effects of the first kitchen remodeling done in 1949, which was not an improvement on the original layout. It still had just the basic appliances and a few feet of counter space crammed into a 10- by 11-ft. kitchen that also had to accommodate an eating table. The little kitchen was stuck between the maid's quarters—they didn't have one—and the rest of the house.

More countertop space is the biggest addition to this new kitchen. The owners chose soapstone tops to create a rough-hewn contrast to the glossy wall tiles. The peninsula that separates the kitchen from the eating area is topped in butcher block, both to reduce any chance that those soapstone counters would read as one black monolith, and to unify it with the floor.

Then they decided to start their family and things had to change. In addition to the maid's quarters—also about 10 feet square—the area behind the kitchen had a laundry room, also about 10 feet square. Expanding beyond the footprint of the original house was out of the question. The space they needed would be cobbled together for three small, square rooms.

Kameron Rutschman of Dorado Designs in Tucson worked out the plan for them. Her design tripled the space available, but the resulting kitchen was long and somewhat narrow—too narrow for an island but too wide for an efficient galley layout. Rutschman's solution was a small peninsula for the food preparation center. Close to the range, this peninsula layout follows Steidl's recommendation that one sink be positioned so that the person working at it can see what's cooking on the range by just turning his or her head.

The peninsula breaks the space into two rooms, eliminating what could have been the bowling-alley effect of a single 28-foot-long by 11-foot-wide open space. It's close to both the refrigerator and a small pantry, provides a set-down area for foods coming out of the microwave, and is a handy serving counter for people eating casual meals at the table.

What's striking about this kitchen are the warm yellow wall tiles and the vibrant colors of

At 10 × 11 feet the old kitchen, inset, wasn't much: a sink under a window, the range on the adjacent counter with a 30-inch cabinet for separation, a refrigerator at the end of the other counter, plus a dishwasher added at the expense of a storage cabinet.

The new kitchen has more than triple the space. It also has the sink—enlarged and improved—under the same window, the only one on that side of the house.

On the Side
Grilling
Vegetables
The Frugal Gourmet's

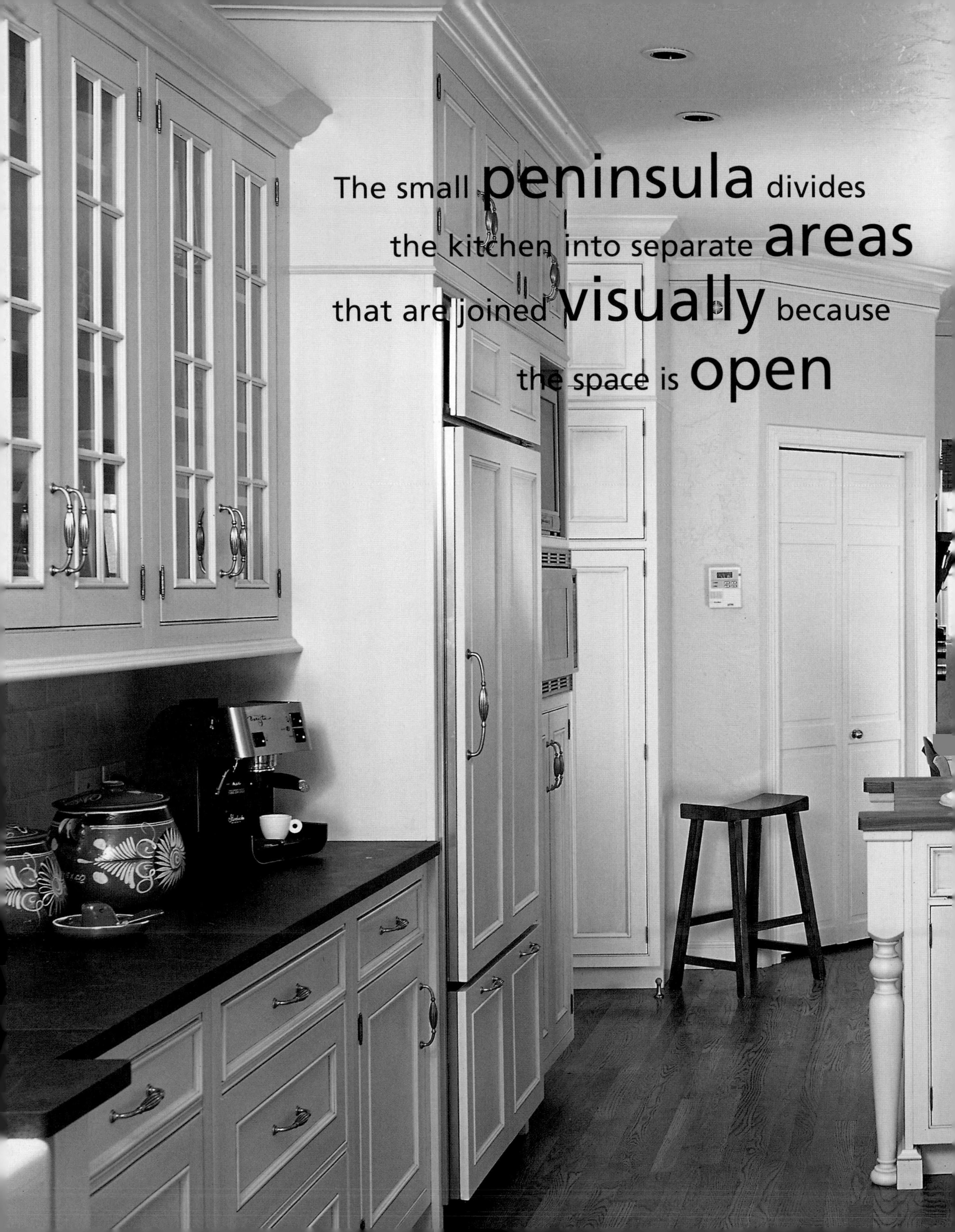

The small **peninsula** divides the kitchen into separate **areas** that are joined **visually** because the space is **open**

the Mexican Talavera pottery on display. The owners had been collecting it for years; some of it was in the old kitchen. Rutschman re-used the old kitchen's display technique—deep shelves above the windows where the pottery could sit securely. To create what looks like a single, continuous display area, she built a shelf out from the chase hiding the range hood ducts. Window treatments are simple: matchstick blinds formed into Roman shades. She didn't want anything to compete with the Talavera. For the same reason, there is only one cabinet on this display wall.

Niches chiseled out of brick walls are common in Tucson. The one added behind the range is similar to others elsewhere in the house dating from the original construction. Both Rutschman and the owners saw it as a big, tactile focal point. And unlike the shallow kitchen niches built with wood frame construction, the double brick walls in the Southwest are deep enough to be used as open storage spaces. That was important here, since there are no wall cabinets close to the range.

From the Designer ▶ To Your Kitchen

SMALL PENINSULAS can effectively divide long, narrow spaces. **WHEN ADDING** an island is out of the question, locate the prep sink as close to the cooking center as possible. **ROUND TABLES** get the most use from a square space, will seat the most people, and won't impede traffic flow around them. **KEEP AN EYE OUT** for small spaces that you can press into service for planning centers or for additional storage areas.

Shallow, open shelves give the owners a place for books and a few more pieces of Mexican pottery. This is a compromise in a kitchen with a cabinet-free wall. While the window shelf impedes access to the books, the alternative would have been no book storage at all.

A well-organized and compact planning center, left, is tucked into an alcove behind the eating table—a good use of space that might have gone unused otherwise. A small corner room holds the new laundry.

Only a round table, below left, could easily fit in the space that Rutschman allowed for an eating area. Space had to be left for people coming through the back door and for access to the laundry room. The 30s-era art deco light fixture above the table previously hung in the dining room.

Positioned flush with the cabinets, the TV, below right, swivels so it can be seen from anywhere in the kitchen.

Life on an Island

Moving is common today, the trend being from a larger house to a smaller one. For some people, though, giving up a well-designed kitchen that has looked great and worked well for many years is a downside to downsizing. Is there a way around this? Yes. Duplicate what you had, even if it's on a smaller scale.

The most likely scenario is to trade a house for a condo or townhouse. Many new condos allow purchasers design options. That was the case here. And the owners of this new Connecticut townhouse took full advantage of their options to recreate features they had long loved. For guidance they turned to architect Louise Brooks of Brooks and Falatico in New Canaan, Connecticut.

With family visiting regularly an open and casual living space was just as important as reproducing the former kitchen. The space Brooks had to work with did not allow for long runs of countertop. Brooks' solution was to design a 4- by 8-foot island as the kitchen's

A symmetrical, furniture-style island divides the kitchen and living area. The island is the primary work surface and a visual stage for the recessed hearth cooking center behind it. More counter space is to the cook's right as she stands at the range. The plate rack, above, is not just for display. Plates kept there are regularly used when family comes over for casual meals.

working focal point. By placing a multi-use sink in the island directly opposite the commercial-style six-burner range, she centralized food preparation, cooking and clean-up in a stand-and-spin arrangement—an efficient design that professional chefs prefer when space is tight. An additional counter and most of the storage areas are built into a wall that is to the right of the range. The microwave is a drawer model—a real convenience to left handers—is below this counter and easily accessible from the work trench formed by the island and the range.

The island is a functional divider separating the kitchen from the living area in this 18- by 20-foot space. Designed like a piece of furniture with decorative brackets and feet, it matches the look of the kitchen storage areas. Brooks designed them to resemble breakfronts.

A casual living area next to the kitchen is a comfortable place for guests who want to be close to the cook. The deep island separates the kitchen from the living area. Inside the island is an entertainment center, inset, with a TV hidden behind a pair of bifold doors.

To Your Kitchen

From the Designer

ISLANDS can be used for things other than cooking and eating. When an island faces a living area consider using it to hide a TV or a full entertainment center. **WHEN SPACE IS TIGHT,** rethink the appliances you buy and where you put them. A satellite work center based on a microwave is a good option.

Refrigerators, above, are just around the corner within convenient reach of the cook at the range or sink. They are also close to the butler's pantry. One of them is used for beverage storage. Freezer drawers are mounted below the refrigerators.

A sink in the butler's pantry, left, anchors a multi-purpose work center for someone preparing drinks and hors d'oeuvres. A second dishwasher handles clean up for glassware and provides overflow capacity when the owners entertain.

The owners' former kitchen had been white and that is what they wanted here. So white predominates as a background color. The counters are fabricated from statuary marble and bright white subway backsplash tiles in the cooking hearth reflect natural light from a large picture window in the living area. Not wanting everything to be white, the owners choose earthtone limestone tiles for the flooring used throughout. Besides adding tonal and textural contrast, the darker flooring is easy to maintain and doesn't show dirt and sand that's tracked in when the family visits and go back and forth between the house and the water.

Carriage lights above the island are decorative—their pale green trim matching the owners' plate collection displayed in the open rack. Task lighting for the island is provided by recessed ceiling fixtures.

The clean white of kitchen walls continues in the adjoining living area. Blue and pale green pastels give both spaces subtle but inviting color accents. Large garden finials on the fireplace mantel also accent the white. Brooks positioned the fireplace so that it can viewed by guests waiting for dinner and by the cook in the kitchen.

Water views are an important part of the design. A divided light picture window is the backdrop for the sofa. Family members sitting there can watch the TV, hidden in the island.

Eyes for the Past

Growing up in Ireland, your ideas about kitchens differ from those of Americans. For one thing, you probably are comfortable with an older look—not a modern-day interpretation of country this or country that, but the timeless elegance of Georgian style that continues to influence design in the British Isles to this day. And when you visualize the kitchen you want, you may see it as groupings of furniture-like pieces rather than runs of base cabinets with wall cabinets above them—what Europeans call an unfitted kitchen look.

Now your home is in Connecticut and that old, remembered look is what you want for your new family kitchen over here. And you like to cook.

The owners of this kitchen began recreating this unfitted look by first hiring a friend who is a retired architect. His plan added a 150-square-foot space to the back of the house, which is where the

The island with a mahogany top is the center of family activity and where the kids sit to help with cooking. The mahogany has been treated with a marine-quality finish to protect it from moisture. Behind the island, to the right of the ovens, is the 48-inch-wide storage pantry. It's made to look like an armoire, in keeping with the European feel the owners wanted.

Meadow Gold Butter

Armour's
STAR
BACON

new kitchen would be. His straightforward layout called for splitting cooking and baking functions between two centers, on opposite sides of the kitchen: an island for food preparation and eating, and a planning center in a transitional space between the kitchen and the new breakfast room. It was a good plan, but to those Irish eyes looking at the elevation drawings, it was too contemporary—too many runs of base cabinets with too many wall cabinets above them. Not at all a look recalling the memory of an old country kitchen.

That's when they turned to Connecticut designer Chris Donner. The owners were clear, Donner remembers: they liked the floorplan and nothing on it would be altered. But they wanted the look changed. Donner did this by suggesting material the owners hadn't thought of: soapstone counters, a mahogany top for the island, subway tiles with a rough, crackle finish. Then she showed them how these materials could be combined with warm wood cabinets made and placed to look like furniture.

Donner began at the island. It was functional and centrally placed but looked like a big box in the center of the kitchen. She suggested giving it an Edwardian look with wainscotted sides, painted off-white to contrast with the cabinets. Adding the mahogany top, the decorative brackets, and bun feet make the island look like a piece of furniture.

Varying colors and textures, from the island sides in wainscotting, to the subway tiles used to surround the range, to the open areas on the wall, give this kitchen the European unfitted look the owners were after. For a bit of whimsy in this Georgian kitchen, they commissioned a very modern kinetic sculpture to hang over the island, which they like to watch turn in the wind.

A different kind of foot—more accurately called furniture cut-out toes—was specified for the cooktop cabinet. Its shelves for pot storage were left open to provide a visual break from the wood-fronted base cabinets on either side of it. Cut-out toes were also used on the sink cabinet. And the only two wall cabinets got glass doors with Georgian mullion bars.

Storage in this kitchen is centralized in a 48-inch-wide, ceiling-height pantry. Donner's decorative touches made it look more like an armoire—eighteenth-century pilasters frame it and the new fronts trick the eye into thinking there are four doors instead of two.

The planning center is next to the storage pantry. The owner had cookbooks she wanted to see; she also had old magazines and school directories she didn't want to see. So Donner designed the center with open shelves directly above the desk for the books and closed cabinets for everything else. In addition to the desk, an old-fashioned pull-out breadboard above the filing drawers provides extra space for laying out bills—but only when needed. One feature in the planning center, not seen often, is a set of cubbies, rather like message boxes in a roll-top desk. There's one for each family member, six of them plus a spare, which, the owner jokes, doesn't indicate that she is about to have another child.

The irregular surfaces on the subway tiles Donner used on the backsplashes and the curved surround over the cooktop—a handmade crackle finish—pick up the pinks, violets, and browns from elsewhere in the kitchen. Inserted into this crackle-finish field tile behind the cooktop are two tile murals designed to look like medieval woodcuts—a design idea that harks back to the eighteenth century.

From the Designer ▶ To Your Kitchen

BUN FEET ON ISLANDS and toe cut outs on base cabinets will give both the look and feel of furniture. **WOOD COUNTERS** are beautiful, but they need to be treated and sealed. A marine finish works best for mahogany and teak. Ask about what's best for other woods. **SOAPSTONE COUNTERS** create a wonderful textural contrast and they wear well. But the only color they come in is black.

The breakfast room, below left, is in the space where the original kitchen used to be.

Contrasting with the black soapstone counters, a white farm sink, far left and opposite, anchors the kitchen's cleanup center.

Pull-out shelves next to the dishwasher, left, are placed at kid height—setting the table and doing the dishes are their jobs. These dish shelves are also near where the family eats.

Seven cubbies built into the planning center, below right—one for each family member, plus a spare—keep family activities organized.

Blue and White

Being a grandfather has its rewards, though you might not think cooking for all the grandchildren—regularly—is one of them. This weekend cooking ritual with the kids determined much of the planning for new kitchen built into the couple's new retirement home. Grandmother's wish for a blue and white kitchen determined the look.

As often happens with new construction, the architect left the kitchen design to someone else: in this case Connecticut-based designer Toni Gallagher. The long, narrow space the architects allotted for the kitchen—with no specific details about what came next—was the only problem Gallagher faced, because the space could neither be altered nor expanded.

Gallagher divided this space between the kitchen and a dining area that, while informal, is not exactly casual. There are four distinct work centers in this kitchen: three on one side of an island

The heart of this kitchen is the cook center with its six-burner cooktop and warming drawer. For convenience the cook has a choice of water sources. Blue and white tiles are used for all the backsplashes and a display shelf above the cooking hearth lets the homeowners show off their collection of blue and white ceramic accessories.

VIKING

Work centers on both sides of
of an island let two cooks
use the kitchen with ease

and one on the other. The cook's work trench is between a six-burner cooktop and a small prep sink in the island. For convenience, and because the grandfather offers choices to the kids that have to stay warm, Gallagher put a warming drawer directly under the cooktop.

The clean-up center is on the other side of the island. Gallagher placed a sink in the middle of a base cabinet run and put dishwashers at both ends of the run—an eye-catching symmetrical arrangement. The symmetry continues with matching refrigerators and freezer drawers flanking the cabinets.

Wall ovens on the cook's side of the kitchen are used more for holiday dinners than for baking. The ovens' stainless steel doors mark the end of the kitchen and the start of the dining area.

With the exception of the cooking appliances all of the kitchen surfaces are blue and white. Creating the look involved more than just Gallagher's time at a drawing board. She spent many days shopping with the grandmother to choose fabrics, flooring, tile, and accessories. This after other trips shopping for appliances to meet current and future cooking needs. To keep these shopping trips from being open-ended Gallagher asked the grandmother to narrow down her selection of choices—to edit the shopping list, as it were—before starting out.

The white cabinets are the background for the blue accents. They were finished and painted on site. Next came the flooring. The owners wanted stone, but settled for large white ceramic tiles with small blue inserts set at a diagonal to the field tile so they would appear diamond shape.

The blue and white decorative theme continues in the dining area. Chairs around the simple country-style table use a checked fabric for their seats. The window treatment is done in blue and white toile, while in the hutch blue and white chinoiserie sit on open shelves. Completing the decor, two prints depicting Chinese Ming dynasty blue and white hang above the hutch.

The clean-up center occupies an entire wall on the other side of the island. High windows above the sink let sunlight stream in. A microwave built into the cook's side of the island is within easy reach of the cooktop. Shallow display bins at both ends of the island are used to show off a collection of shells.

Because of the kids running in and out of the house, Gallagher suggested a durable indoor/outdoor fabric for the chair seats. This makes these well-used seats easy to clean and long lasting.

For the backsplashes Gallagher chose a white field tile with small blue decorations in the corners. Then she picked four decorative tiles, each depicting a different flower, and arranged them on an alternating basis. The result give the backsplashes the look of a tile mural. The tile also coordinates with the collection of Delft blue and white vases that sit on a display shelf above the cooking hearth.

To Your Kitchen

From the Designer

KITCHEN DESIGNERS do more than draw plans. Ask them to help shop for products. They'll do it gladly. **EDIT YOUR SHOPPING LIST** before you go. Don't spend time looking at products you know you won't buy. **CHAIR FABRICS** made for indoor/outdoor use are a good choice if an eating area will be used regularly by children.

A big, cold-water spigot, above, is a convenience serious cooks should consider. Even with a water source at the nearby prep sink, this spigot makes filling pasta pots much easier. The spigot used here swivels in all directions and easily reaches pots on any of the burners.

Gallagher created a planning center on a small wall opposite the head of the table. The desk chair, along with another chair, shown on the opposite page, can be used at the table when there are eight guests.

Bay Area Beckons

Saturday morning in the hills above Berkeley, California. Mark Kendall stands at his 60-inch, custom-made cooktop and griddle, ready for some short-order cooking as his kids and their sleepover friends wander in for a hearty breakfast.

As a builder and developer, Mark understood how to create the structure for what he and his wife Jane wanted—a kitchen under a seven-sided cupola that has been fashioned from steel beams clad in reclaimed lumber. Arsenio Perez Jr., CKD, from KB Associates in San Mateo, California, the area WoodMode dealer, helped Jane Kendall work out the efficient kitchen under that cupola. Actually, Perez helped both Kendalls since they wanted different and potentially contradictory features.

Mark wanted more than a wet bar, he wanted something approaching a real bar. "For us, this kitchen was to be a place where we could spend most of our time, a place to entertain in a convivial,

A full-service bar is the centerpiece of this kitchen, which comes alive when family and friends arrive for food and fun. From his spot inside the bar, Mark Kendall—literally in the center of things—gets the party going while his wife Jane prepares the meal in the work trench running along two of the island's four sides.

private bar atmosphere with the kitchen right next to it."

Jane Kendall wanted to cook.

Perez devised a plan that worked for both of them. The island, in the shape of a hollow square, has plenty of room for Kendall to be a bartender. Everything for a well-equipped bar is there: small sink; a pure water dispenser; a cooler for beer, soda and wine; and plenty of storage space for glassware and accessories.

For Jane's part of the kitchen—the cooking part—Perez laid out an L-shaped work trench that lets her move easily from the major centers built into both sides of it. He put the refrigerator, the freezer, and two refrigerator drawers for fresh produce at the corner of the L. Across from these, on the corner of the island, he put the prep sink, which is where Jane normally works when the couple entertains. Its location lets Jane talk with guests sitting at the island.

Perez also put a pantry at the corner of the L, which together with the refrigerators and freezer, forms the kitchen's centralized storage center. Before remodeling, that space had been a hallway leading to the kids' bedrooms. "Hey wait a minute," Jane recalls saying. "What I don't need is for kids to be funneled directly into the part of the kitchen where I work." She did need a pantry. So the plan was changed.

Positioned directly under the cupola with its seven-sided skylight, the bar and the kitchen get natural light at any time of day. The bar's wood serving counter was matched with the height of the bar stools for the comfort of the guests. On the bar's other side, the granite counters are a standard height for easy food preparation.

Diamond-shaped tiles, right, in four bright colors, create a mosaic backsplash behind the cooktop. The pot filler, mounted above the left bank of burners, is another convenience for southpaws.

A large farm sink, opposite page, handles cleanup chores. To the left of it is a dishwasher drawer, placed in that side because Jane Kendall is left-handed.

The open plate rack, below right, is for everyday dishes—dishes whose bright yellow fits with the kitchen color scheme established by the tile work.

Serving counters at the bar are wood, in keeping with the feel the owners wanted. The island work surfaces are granite.

Jane Kendall is left-handed.

Perez took this into account in working out appliance placement. The 60-inch cooktop comes with the bank of four burners on the left side. The left-hand position of the pot filler makes this setup even more convenient. For the baking center, Perez placed the wall ovens as far to the right as possible to create a set-down area to the left of them that Jane could use conveniently. One of the dishwashers, a drawer model, is at the left of the cleanup sink. Jane uses this one. Two more dishwasher drawers are to the right of the sink—her kids are right-handed and she wanted to make it easy for them to do the dishes.

Besides the bar in the center of the kitchen, what grabs your eye is the tile above the cooktop. Jane wanted an eye-catching tile design for the backsplash and hood, but couldn't decide colors. So she picked them all: diamond-shaped tiles in four bright impact colors. Her husband calls these colors the California Tuscany blend. Playful. The same blend of bright colors forms the backsplash under the open plate rack.

The chase hiding the hood and ductwork is pure yellow and runs to the ceiling. But this big yellow "chimney" also has the effect of lowering the perception of ceiling height which, as Mark says, helps bring the ceiling details down to eye level. Another trick Mark used to cut the perceived distance between the ceiling and counters was to install extra-tall wall cabinets and then to use the space on top of them to display big items such as large platters and baskets. The big clock above the sink also scales back the space.

From the Designer

To Your Kitchen

LEFT-HANDED? Then make sure to tell your designer that you want countertop layouts that favor your left side, like left-oriented setdown areas next to the cooktop and range, and dishwashers placed to the left of the sink. **ISLANDS ARE CONVERSATIONAL MAGNETS.** If you entertain regularly and have the space, think about an island large enough to accommodate stools to make it easy for guests to hang out. **DON'T BE AFRAID** of bright colors. They can add interest to your kitchen and help unify big spaces.

Shakespeare

4

Kitchens for Parties

Kitchens go public when you entertain. In the 21st century, kitchens will be flexible enough to move effortlessly and quickly from being the focus of family activities to the life of the party.

WOLF

Entertain Anytime

What makes a kitchen the life of the party? What does a kitchen designed for entertaining need in order to do it well? For New Canaan, Connecticut architect Judy Larson that's simple: a big island, plenty of room to move around, and lots of dishwashers to make cleanup easy. When Larson and her husband, Bill Gardiner, a builder, got an opportunity to remodel a house for themselves from the ground up, she had a chance to put her ideas into practice for her most demanding client—herself.

Larson started by giving herself plenty of space to work with: an 18- by 19-foot-9-inch area for the kitchen. This was more than enough to hold the 8-by 10-foot island she wanted and still have room for passageways around and through the kitchen.

Besides wanting to provide a generous work surface for kitchen tasks normally done at an island, Larson saw this island as a big table in the middle of her kitchen—like a nineteenth century

The cooking center has a small commercial-style range with a closeby sink. Opposite the range, on the island, are a wok burner and a steamer, both counter-mounted and accessible to the cook simply by turning around. While the range has an oven, most of the baking and roasting are done in the ovens located in the butler's pantry. That's where the microwave is.

scullery table—big enough for several cooks and helpers, first to prepare meals for twenty or thirty people, then to serve them buffet style to her guests. As if that weren't enough, she designed a curved breakfast bar on one side of it and a built-in love seat facing a fireplace, on the other.

When not entertaining, Larson uses her island as a visual focal point in the house, with displays that catch the spirit of the changing seasons: pumpkins in the fall, festive Christmas decorations, then tulips in the spring. "You need a big island for this, especially if you're going to use it for cooking at the same time."

Larson's kitchen works in partnership with the 8 × 13 ft. walk-through butler's pantry she designed next to it. The pantry has a sink, a dishwasher, two freezer drawers, plus as much work counter space as in the kitchen itself. Here, too, she put the microwave and the wall ovens. One benefit of duplicating prep and cleanup centers in the pantry is to spread the work areas out so that people don't get in each other's way when getting things ready for a party.

Larson designed the butler's pantry with summer entertaining in mind; it joins the kitchen with a long covered porch. Cleaning up from summer parties happens here. The mess doesn't migrate to the kitchen.

Throughout the design process, cleanup was on Larson's mind. Her approach to this aspect of

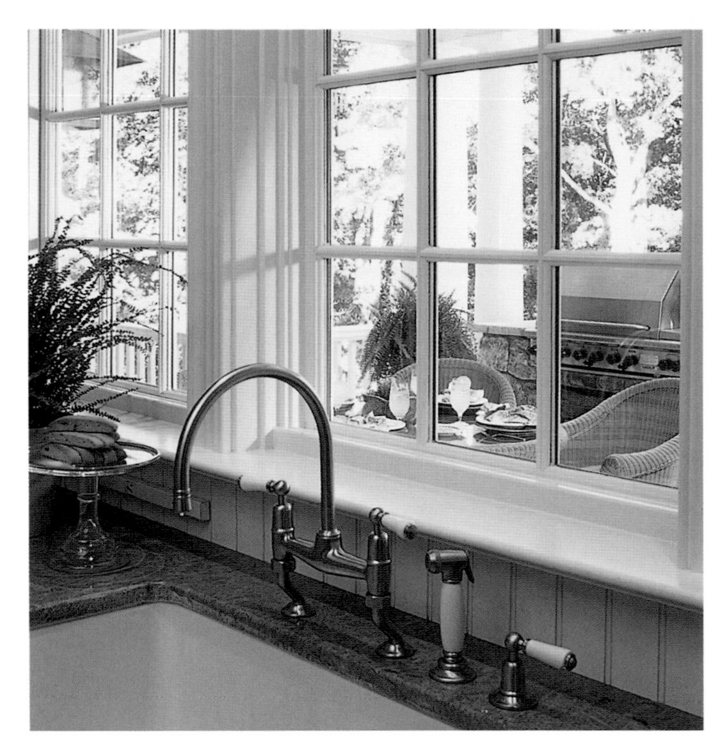

The butler's pantry, opposite page, links the kitchen to both a big summer porch, above, and the formal dining room. Plenty of counter space here means room for plating party meals and handling dirty dishes after the party. The wall ovens turn the pantry into a cooking and baking center. Placing the large sink, top and opposite page, and dishwasher next to them, localizes cleanup from both the indoor and outdoor dining areas.

WOLF
WOLF
This home is blessed
with family, friends,
laughter, love, and dogs.

kitchen design is planned versatility. Besides wanting lots of dishwashers—there are three—she suggests having more than one cleanup sink. "Many people like to engage guests in the process—not just meal preparation, but also cleanup." More than one sink means more than one place where this can happen. Someone can clean up, keeping ahead of the mess—with the help of a guest, of course—while others continue with the food preparation.

This happens often at the twin farm sinks that form Larson's primary cleanup center. She sees these twin sinks as a very large double bowl sink—very large. Pots can soak in one sink while vegetables are washed in the other. A sink arrangement like this, she points out, is also a good place to bathe a small dog, perhaps one in each sink, if you have two.

Larson specified base cabinets, with deep drawers. She prefers drawer storage for keeping nonperishable boxed foods and finds them easier to use than cabinets with roll-out shelves, especially when equipped with self-closing hardware. Her wall cabinets are deeper than the standard 13 inches in order to accommodate large

Talk about a big island. This one has built-in seating that faces a kitchen fireplace. Larson wanted it big because she saw it as a multi-use table. When she and her husband entertain, it's where the smorgasbord goes. Wide spaces between the island and the counters make it easy for guests to move around and not feel crowded as they graze the food. When she does not use the island for parties, Larson likes to display seasonal items on it.

A sunlit octagonal breakfast room is an inviting space for family meals or a casual get-together with another couple. For those larger parties, the table is another serving station. A door leads to the covered porch, providing easy access to cool outdoor seating for people who have been through the buffet line.

platters. What about the trend away from wall cabinets? That's fine, she says, for contemporary styles or when you want a lot of windows in your kitchen. "But I think some things just store better in wall cabinets—coffee mugs, for example."

So do Larson's space-planning ideas work? One of her first parties proved that they do. She prepared a buffet supper for forty. Guests moved effortlessly around the island and the small breakfast table, helping themselves to entrees. Then it was on to the dessert bar in the butler's panty.

When it was over, both kitchen and pantry cleaned up well.

To Your Kitchen

From the Designer

DISHWASHERS. Put in as many as you have space for. You'll use them all the time and won't regret it. **SINKS,** the same thing: Three are better than two. Pick ones with big, deep bowls—good for soaking large pots and small dogs. **DEEP DRAWERS** store packaged food, as well as cookware. Drawers work better than base cabinets with pull-out shelves and, if you've got kids, use self-closing hardware. **13-INCH-DEEP** wall cabinets may not be deep enough for big platters, so have them made a little deeper.

The stone fireplace, top right, used every day in the winter, is a focal point for the kitchen.

Twin sinks, top left, let the cooks keep up with cleanup chores in one bowl, while using the other one for food preparation.

A small planning desk, right, gives Larson a spot near the fire where she can organize her parties.

Friendly Formality

"I wanted a place to slice my bread," one of the owners said to Connecticut designer Mary Jo Peterson, CKD. It was just one of quite a few things on the list for improving a dated kitchen in a 1720s house.

It took Peterson two tries before she understood that these owners were less interested in space planning and more interested in how the new space felt. "What turned out to be important," Peterson remembers, "was the character of the kitchen, the parameters of the people using the space, not the space itself." This is not to say that making the space work efficiently wasn't important; it was. But it was complicated by a staircase that couldn't be moved. It was going to be smack in the middle of any new design Peterson drew.

The owners are great cooks. Often, they'll call friends on a Friday afternoon and ask them over to taste-test a new recipe they're

Placing the commercial-style range at a 45-degree angle breaks up a long wall that could easily look like a railroad siding. By pointing the range toward the eating table, the kitchen merges seamlessly into the eating area, effectively unifying them into one space in which people move from cooking to conversation when the meal is served.

A custom-made **furniture** piece **disguises** a stairwell that couldn't be moved

trying out. What they wanted was a friendly, open kitchen in which they could cook together with guests and then sit down together to enjoy the meal with wine and good conversation.

Peterson's plan for this called for keeping the food preparation, baking, and cooking centers on the right side of the staircase. There is a large, dual-purpose sink on this side of the kitchen, along with a dishwasher for pots and pans. On the other side of the staircase, she installed a sink and dishwasher specifically for dishes, glassware, and silver: items stored in this part of the kitchen.

This was the bones of the plan. Fleshing it out, creating the character of the kitchen was the job of cabinet maker Sam Cousins. Cousins is the late Julia Childs' nephew. He remembered the times he spent in her kitchen, a memory that taught him that kitchen design has as much to do with making the kitchen part of the lives of those who use it as it does with choosing the right appliances.

Cousins likened the big staircase to a 500-pound elephant in the kitchen that you couldn't shoo away. He suggested that the owners accentuate it; call attention to it, not as a staircase but as a piece of furniture. They agreed. Cousins dressed it with tiger maple. Depending on how you view it, it looks like it could be a walk-in pantry, or perhaps a free-standing storage and display unit. Doors leading to the stairs are false fronts designed to look like drawers below a cabinet. Continuing the furniture idea, Cousins built two tables that face into the kitchen's cooking area. The butternut cabinets, painted, sanded and painted again for a distressed look, were also handmade by Cousins.

So what about the character everyone was after—those people parameters? "Well," say the owners, "we have cocktails in the kitchen, everyone helps cook, then we sit down for an intimate dinner. After that, when we're well-fed, you fill up both dishwashers and go to bed."

That's my idea of a good party.

From the Designer

To Your Kitchen

IF YOU CAN'T CHANGE something in your kitchen, think about disguising it—turn it into a visual focal point. Like turning a lemon into lemonade. **LOOK CLOSELY** at small, apparently useless spaces. You may be able to use them for display areas. **GROUP YOUR** work centers into work zones that take into account traffic flow through the kitchen. **THE RIGHT SPACE** plan is only one half of kitchen design. Accessories and decorative details make a new kitchen match your personality.

Made from the same tiger maple used to disguise the stairway, the accessory table, opposite page, adds to the idea that this kitchen is a collection of fine furniture.

A cleanup and storage area for dishes and glasses, left, is used for additional prep space and for party hors d'oeuvres. The shallow plate display shows how a tough space can be put to good use.

The large planning center, below left, sits between the cooking center and the table where casual meals are eaten.

A service bar, below right, is the cocktail center for both the kitchen and dining room. Under the poster is a formal eating area for the owners' two standard poodles.

European Vision

A white canvas for the art on the walls, the furnishings in the rooms, and the visual impact of the kitchen. This is very European—not the Americanized version of a European look, but a close replica of a Belgian manor house, or perhaps a French country house on the Mediterranean. It's exactly what the owner, a European businessman, wanted and what builder Frederick Allen and kitchen designer Julia Zemp gave him.

The kitchen is intentionally sparse to call attention to its two focal points: a French range, made by the same company that provided painter Claude Monet with one in 1908, and the radius window above the sink. It was custom-made to match the interior archways and separate the first-floor rooms.

What strikes you first in this kitchen is how white the walls are. They are white-washed plaster, the plaster hand-applied to create an imperfect, rustic finish. But unlike plaster walls in old European

A crisp white plaster wall with oak accents and accessories results in a kitchen with a simple, but eye-catching color scheme. The radius of the arch above the pass-through, which links the kitchen and dining room, was selected by trial and error. The same radius curve is used on the kitchen window and on the deep niches in the pantry.

homes, these walls have been sealed to prevent them from becoming chalky. Two other features the owner insisted on—in fact, he provided the material for them—are the hand-planed ceiling beams, imported from France, and the floor, made from 300-year-old roof tiles salvaged from French villas and refinished for use in this manner.

With these pure white walls as a backdrop, the owner wanted a kitchen that looked as though it had been there for a hundred years. Kitchen designer Zemp knew exactly what he was after. Her British background made it easy for her to visualize and design a historic European kitchen.

"I was given a U-shape layout by the architect, and the owner had picked the French range and decided on the other appliances. My job was so much in space planning, as to give this kitchen more visual interest by using level changes and moving the eye back and forth by using niches in the walls."

There are no base cabinets as Americans think of them. Instead, quarter-sawn drawers are fitted into the white plaster walls. The sink cabinet is more like a piece of old oak furniture. Zemp had it built 2 inches higher than the surrounding countertops, specifically to set it apart and make it look like an antique slid into a spot that had been left open for it.

A small kitchen table the owner imported from France is the kitchen's centerpiece—literally. Placed almost dead center, it becomes the element that unifies the legs of the U-shape kitchen. It adds to the European manor house feel the owner wanted, and, of course, it's a functional work surface.

Open niches, white-washed plaster walls, and natural oak are elements of true European design

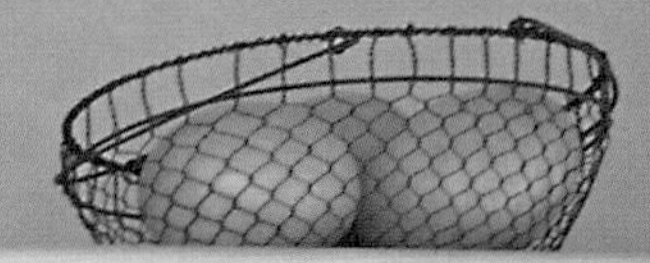

From the Designer

To Your Kitchen

ANTIQUES ADD a lot to a kitchen, so don't be afraid to use them—not just small things you display, but larger items like tables, that you use. **SMALL SPACES,** especially if they are in corners, too often are relegated to open tray storage. Try something different, a built-in that's both functional and looks good.

The dining room, above left, is connected to the kitchen by a pass-through.

Both appealing to the eye and an innovative use of a small space, the custom-made storage space built into a base cabinet, above right, holds two trays that are ready to use. These trays were also custom-made to fit the spaces where they would be stored.

While not exactly a full-fledged planning center, this phone and message alcove, left, built into the pantry, is a convenient place to keep track of lists.

The French-made range, above left, is finished in white to be consistent with the kitchen's color scheme. Behind it, Zemp chose white tile to match the statuary marble countertops.

Attached to the side of the kitchen table is a brass rail, above right, with hooks from which towels and other items can hang in a ready-to-use location.

There are no wall cabinets either. Zemp remembers her client saying to her that he didn't want any because, "all you do is store rubbish in them. If you have them, you accumulate more rubbish." There are, however, three open shelves, there to provide a visual break from the white walls as much to give the owner a place to display some old pottery.

Some of what might be kept in wall cabinets is stored on open shelves on the refrigerator wall and niches above it. These shelves were Zemp's idea. To the left of the refrigerator—itself disguised as an armoire—Zemp took a foot of space that could easily have been left blank and made shelves. Her mixing of oak and plaster repeats the motif used elsewhere in the kitchen. In the pantry, the deep niches are possible because the walls are thicker than normal. Niches in the pantry, these with the same radius arch of the kitchen window, are high enough for tall books and deep enough for small appliances.

In Good Company

Halloween is Ellen Dickson's favorite holiday and favorite reason to have a party. A Chicago architect, she's spent years designing kitchens for others while leaving her own kitchen "as is." When the ongoing remodeling of her 1940s-era house got around to the kitchen, she had the opportunity to try the ideas her clients had rejected as a bit too far out.

Dickson's kitchen isn't large, nor is the dining room that opens onto it. Adding space to either room wasn't in the plans, so it was a question of rearranging the space she had to make it more efficient for herself, for her family, and for the parties that regularly fill up her kitchen with friends. In her mind, too, Dickson wanted a kitchen that, well, didn't exactly look like a kitchen.

What does a non-kitchen kitchen look like? No wall cabinets for starters. Dickson specifically wanted something other than what she calls the boom, boom, boom of a row of wall cabinets staring

The kitchen hutch, sometimes with Nikkita the cat holding court, is the first thing people see when they enter the kitchen. Dickson designed it as a piece of furniture whose lower doors recall turn-of-the-twentieth-century pie safes. The stained glass window was bought in England; Dickson attributes its perfect fit in the window to plain good luck.

A small kitchen feels
larger if it has
no wall cabinets

out at you. So her new kitchen doesn't have any. The immediate result is that the room feels bigger and is less claustrophobic.

But about storage—all the stuff that every kitchen has? It has to go somewhere. Pantries are one alternative, and Dickson set out to design one that was interesting and stored a lot. "However, I don't like full-depth pantries. They're too solid and too imposing." This led her to try an idea she'd been suggesting to clients without much success—a dovecote storage wall.

The dovecote she designed takes up the entire wall to the left of the refrigerator. It has nine storage cubbies with doors mounted on hardware that lets them flip up and hide inside the cubby. "We had enough counter space to do what we wanted," Dickson said. "But in a pinch, doors on the lower cubbies can be flipped up to give us more." The granite counters run under them.

Dickson's second alternative to wall cabinets is a large hutch she designed to look like a piece of furniture. She built it around an existing window and placed it so that guests coming in the front door look directly at it—their first impression of the kitchen. The hutch separates the kitchen and dining room; Dickson uses it to store items used in both rooms.

The island is the heart of this kitchen. Dickson kept the prep sink small because she wanted as much counter area as possible. This is where she puts the party appetizers and where people sit—on the stools until they are all taken, then on the island. Party guests also sit on the counters running along the kitchen's perimeter. Another advantage of no wall cabinets.

A storage wall, in the form of a dovecote, substitutes for wall cabinets, which Dickson didn't want. Doors to the cubbies lift up and slide back out of the way. The door design repeats the pie-safe motif used in the hutch.

CLASSICO
Imagine
ORGANIC
CREAMY BUTTERNUT SQUASH
Imagine
ORGANIC
CREAMY TOMATO SOUP
CANTUCCINI
SAPORI
Nocciola
Peter Pan
CHICKEN NOODLE SOUP
LONDON
Extra Crisp
English Muffins
2:09

To Your Kitchen

From the Designer

GO WITH THINGS that catch your eye. Don't be afraid to mix styles. **LOOK FOR ALTERNATIVES** to wall cabinets—a hutch or some other piece of furniture that can be used for storage. **DON'T AVOID COLOR.** Real estate agents like white because it's not risky at resale time. But they don't have to live in your kitchen, you do. **CREATE KITCHEN FOCAL POINTS** with color changes, appliance placements, or art work and displays. **DON'T BE AFRAID** to make a mistake. You can fix it in a few years.

The island, left, is the kitchen's primary food preparation center, with the prep sink close to both the storage wall and the refrigerator. The oven in the island is a "quick cook" unit designed to cook food that shouldn't be microwaved,

A big collector of folk art, Dickson put a hand-made sequined crow and rabbit, top right, on the counter where she can enjoy them.

A colorful kitchen was also on Dickson's mind. "I wanted to play with colors people might not be familiar with. For me they are happy colors." This led her to a butternut squash finish for the cabinets, which play off of yellow subway tiles for the kitchen walls. The blue walls in the dining room contrast with these happy colors, with the white hutch acting as a transition element between the rooms.

Then there's the art—the plates on the range hood and the sequined rabbit and crow in the corner near the sink, plus the prints in the dining room. There's just enough so the people enjoying a party in these rooms get the point that life is fun.

The dining room doubles as another buffet for parties starting in the kitchen and moving through the dining room to the backyard patio. The lights over the table are '50s retro; the prints date from the '40s and were made by the same company that made posters for the Grand Ole Opry in Nashville.

Girard

Movable Feast

How about a cooking center that's not in a kitchen? Why not. For a long time, Teri wanted a pizza oven. She also wanted a fireplace with a raised hearth in her kitchen, or at least a fireplace that she could see from her kitchen.

If there had been any doubt about how this kitchen was going to look it vanished when architect Alan Shope, AIA, gave Teri a slice of pizza from his own pizza oven. "We need to do something like this," was all Teri could say.

The 20- by 25-foot space encompassing the kitchen and the fireplace room, let's call it, was added to an existing house. The space planning began with the fireplace.

Many of the smaller stones used to face the chimney flue came from Teri's property. Some of the larger ones were picked out when Teri and Shope walked through Shope's property in Northwest Connecticut, and the really big stones came from project architect

The massive stone hearth and chimney with its firebox and pizza oven are a functional backdrop for casual meals prepared and served at the all-purpose table. Perhaps best called the "casual cooking center," the pizza oven and table are directly opposite the more commonly thought-of work centers, which are in and behind a large island.

Task lighting over the island runs from one side of the kitchen to the other

Erik Freno's land in nearby Amenia, New York.

While the stonemason had done plenty of fireplaces, this was going to be his first pizza oven. Add to this was Teri's wish that the oven be adjacent to the fireplace's firebox and that the large hearth would transition to become the floor of the pizza oven. Oh, and Teri didn't want it to appear that mortar had been used anywhere.

To balance off the fireplace Teri and Shope built a more traditional cooking center around a six-burner, twin-oven commercial-style range. Above it is a soapstone backsplash surmounted with a dark copper range hood. This gives the room a symmetrical balance and establishes the two dark focal points in a room where light tonal values predominate.

The do-everything work space for Teri's kitchen is big, deep island with a single sink. The island is big, not only to provide counter space and to match the scale of the large room, but also because of Teri's decision not to use wall cabinets. The long run of base cabinets and drawers on the fireplace side of the room more than makes up for the storage space wall cabinets would have provided.

Shope found the wood used for the Shaker-inspired cabinets and the flooring at a lumber yard specializing in sustainable products. He then had the wood milled in a local shop.

Back at the fireplace, making and cooking the pizza is a one-stop operation. Teri's husband found the big work table at an antique store. The family rolls out the pizza dough on it and then tuck into a wonderfully informal meal at the same table when the pizza comes hot out of the oven—which is within easy.

A part of the original house, the dining area beyond the kitchen, left, had once been part of a barn silo. The round form was kept and the space is now used primarily for wine-tasting parties. The small serving table, above, is used to display the wines about to be tasted.

Soapstone is used on the kitchen counters and for the backsplash in back of the commercial-style range. The dark patina finish on the copper range hood is a symmetrical counterpoint to the fireplace and chimney on the opposite side of the room. It also helped the light oak base cabinets stand out as a design element.

Big open rooms always look great during the day with sunlight streaming in. To make this kitchen look as just as good when the sun goes down Shope put lighting in the ceiling trusses. These trusses, which give the room structural support and hang below the vaulted ceiling, are channeled. In the channels are concealed lights that shine onto the ceiling. The ceiling vaults act like a big reflector, directing soft light back down on the living spaces.

One thing that's not in this kitchen is a microwave. But then there isn't likely to be any leftover pizza to reheat.

To Your Kitchen

From the Designer

MATERIALS—in this case the fireplace stone—are often close at hand if you look for them. **COOKING CENTERS,** like wetbars, can work outside of a typical kitchen layout. Push the envelope a bit if this is what you want. **NO WALL CABINETS** gives any space a more open feel. The best way to make up for lost storage space is to plan a long run of base cabinets in an island.

Incorporating two flues, the fireplace and pizza oven. above, can operate simultaneously. Open areas for wood storage are cut into the massive hearth.

A coffee bar, built into a storage wall, above right, is accessible from both the island and the fireplace.

Two comfortable chairs flanking a table, right, form a conversational grouping where guests can enjoy the fireplace before moving to the table to eat pizza.

5

Kitchens for Cooks

Ah, cooking. A tasty way to relax for many of us. In the 21st century, new appliances will open up limitless possibilities, and new kitchens will be designed to increase the joy of cooking for one cook or several.

SPAIN
NIGELLA EXPRESS
COOKBOOK

Kitchen Online

I'm short. Libraries have ladders to reach high book shelves. Why can't I have one to reach the high cabinets?" That was Janet's first thought as the new kitchen took shape in her mind's eye. Her mind's eye saw something else, too: "We wanted an old stove." It turned out to be a really old stove. "And we wanted to use lots of recycled wood and have open shelves for storage." Somewhat out of the ordinary for a 21st century kitchen.

Several designers said they didn't think they could put all the elements together. Among them was Randy O'Kane, CKD, of Bilotta Kitchens in Mamaroneck, New York. Happily she re-considered. Her design expertise plus Janet's push-the-envelope ideas and a lot of internet research made this New Jersey kitchen happen.

O'Kane convinced Janet to rethink how old wood might work in the kitchen, explaining that cabinetmakers might not be able to use the wood in the way Janet wanted. O'Kane also told her that

Keeping seasonal items in out-of-the-way places is part of any good storage plan. Often, though, little thought is given to reaching these items when you want them. In this kitchen, with its 10-foot ceilings, the library ladder is the safest way up to get what you need. Another safety feature is the sliding cabinet doors instead a head-bumping swinging door.

open shelving would make it impossible to take advantage of many convenient storage features, such as pullout pantries, that are common accessories for wall cabinets.

Janet agreed but insisted that some open shelving be kept and that the wall cabinets she now accepted should look like they came from a 1930s' scullery kitchen—the look she saw in her far-seeing mind's eye.

What O'Kane came up with can only be described as three kitchens in one. She designed each of the wall elevations differently: The wall backing the stove, shown in the photo at the right, O'Kane made to look like a built-in breakfront. There are only 36 inches of counter space, but that's enough for a safe set-down area for hot pans coming off the stove and for some extra prep surface in case the work counter directly across from the stove fills up. Cabinet doors and drawer fronts are finished with recessed panels. Doors are trimmed with old fashioned latch hardware; drawers open with bin pulls.

The elevation with the library ladder not surprisingly looks like a library. Doors and drawer fronts below the high glass sliding doors are finished with raised panels and trimmed with knobs.

The 14-foot-long island has a 7-foot section of teak boards salvaged from an old train car. This table-height section is for baking and the kids can eat or do homework on it. The island's ends, at counter height, are topped with Pyrolave, an engineered stone made from volcanic ash. These are the kitchen's prep centers. Janet used the internet to find Maurice Jonker, a Florida craftsman, who combined new and old materials to make the island look like furniture from a 1930s' farm.

Chambers

The antique Chambers stove, restored to working order with its enamel refinished in retro green, was one of the starting points from which this kitchen grew.

A modern farm sink with two old-fashioned faucets, top, also goes retro thanks to the wooden base and legs made for it by Mauric Jonker. The green curtain places this 21st century sink center firmly in the 1930s.

Beadboard backing, behind the high shelves on the library ladder wall create a textural contrast to the rest of the kitchen and set a nice stage for the display of books and collectibles.

On the sink wall, Janet got the open shelving she wanted. It's used exclusively for dishes. Placed on both sides of a twin-bowl farm sink, these shelves establish the kitchen's clean-up center and follow the rule that items should be stored as closely as possible to the point of first or last use.

Then there's the ceiling. O'Kane feels ceilings can be an important kitchen design element, but that they are overlooked because people seldom gaze upward. "A kitchen ceiling full of recessed light fixtures can easily look like a Swiss cheese controlled by a switch," she says. Janet had a tin ceiling in mind from the beginning, so there was total agreement.

The centerpiece of this kitchen is a Chambers stove, dating from the 1930s. Janet found it in a church basement in Arizona through an internet auction site. She used the 'net again to find a restorer of old stoves—in Kansas—to make the burners operational again and to refinish the worn-out white enamel in retro green. The restorer drove the Chambers to New Jersey and assembled it on site.

The stove's new green finish determined the color scheme for the floor and also the way color became a design element in the rest of the kitchen. To work out color usage, Janet turned to Architect Tom Conway, AIA. He determined the design of the floor along with the coordinating wall and cabinet colors. You have to look closely at the floor to see that it's new oak planking. The textured green painting completely hides the wood grains and results in a look that seems to combine wood and very large tile.

The final 1930s' touch was a modern fridge trimmed to look like an icebox. The built-in refrigerator and freezer went for over a year with no door panels while Janet searched for the right way to get the look she wanted. Her original idea was a white enamel panel in a stainless steel frame, but she couldn't find one. As an alternative he had the panel and frame made from wood and painted them to match the cabinets. What makes this compromise work is the reproduction icebox door hardware—you guessed it, found on line.

This kitchen gets a workout—lots of cooking for lots of family gatherings. It harkens back to the way kitchens were used early in the twentieth century. The Chambers stove, with its six burners, grill, and two ovens, is the kitchen's primary appliance. The deep soup cooker, a trademark of these old stoves, works overtime. Twice a year, Janet competes in the Soup-Off at her local firehouse. She wins.

What does a 1930s' kitchen built new in the first decade of the 21st century tell us about design and function? One thing, perhaps, is that old ideas aren't always outdated. Randy O'Kane puts it this way: "You're not going to find everything you want to do in the pages of a magazine. Sometimes you have to make a leap of faith." Sometime that leap is backwards.

From the Designer ▶ To Your Kitchen

ON LINE SHOPPING is not just for finding good deals. It is a resource that can expand your design options. **FOLLOW YOUR DREAMS** and don't let a designer tell you something cannot be done. With patience you will find a desginer who will do it your way. **DON'T BE AFRAID OF BRIGHT COLORS** even unusal ones. Color can add wonderful visual focal points to any kitchen. **FLOOR DESIGNS** don't have to be limited to what you can buy in a store. Faux painters can turn your floor into whatever it is you see in your mind.

Shelves for plates, opposite left, are convenient to the sink, fridge and island—and to the kids who use them.

Cubby drawers, left, are used to sort sliverware—and to teach Janet's two young children about table setting. Plaques with initial capital letters tell the kids that big items go here, soup spoons, dinner knives. Lower case letters are for salad forks and teaspoons.

The painted areas of the floor, below left, in faux finish replicate the look of large tile.

A modern sink mounted in a piece of furniture and trimmed with a curtain adds to the 1930s' feel the home owner wanted.

VIKING
PROFESSIONAL

American Nostalgia

How do you design a kitchen with a perfect space plan, find places for dream appliances two demanding cooks want, build in every kind of storage convenience, offer the choice of two places to eat—and still give the kitchen flexibility to accommodate things you might want in the future but haven't thought about yet?

Good question.

Sarah Blank, CKD, of SBD kitchens in Darien, Connecticut, mulled this question over many times as she planned her own new kitchen. As in the old tale about the shoemaker, she has been a professional kitchen designer for 28 years, yet this was the first chance to do for herself what she had been doing for others.

Blank sees herself as a 19th-century person, so designing a kitchen that captured the look and feel of a classic New England home would have been her natural inclination even if she hadn't been an ardent collector of antiques from that period.

Butternut wood cabinets, distressed on site and finished with a glaze, give the kitchen the rural rustic New England flavor Sarah Blank wanted. The work table fits perfectly into the plan, as if by design. In fact, it's an antique Blank bought after the kitchen was done. Another antique, the 13-star flag, above, dates from the 1890s and once adorned the stern of a large boat.

Her kitchen, which grew out of a smaller one by means of an addition, has three important work centers. A six-burner restaurant-style range establishes the cooking along one wall. On the opposite wall, twin sinks and a dishwasher, hidden behind a cabinet panel, form the clean-up center. Between them, an island with a second set of sinks can only be called the kitchen command center—never mind that design books don't have such a term.

Blank had intended this island to be the kitchen's clean-up center. To make that cleaning up as easy as possible she mounted a high-riser, professional spigot above a larger and deeper sink—an ideal set-up for cleaning pots and pans. A big dishwasher within easy reach of the sink should have left no doubt about how the island was going to be used.

It didn't turn out that way when Blank and her husband Charles began using the new kitchen. "Yes, we still clean the big pots there, but that island has become the prep center for the kitchen," said Blank. More than that, it is a well-used serving center for the casual dining area just beyond the island; it's where the many dinner parties Sarah and Charles host get started.

The island's site-built Verde Vecchio granite sink has two bowls. Besides the bigger one for those dirty pots, there's a smaller one, a trough sink. When the entertaining starts, the trough gets filled with ice and becomes a cooler for canned and bottled beverages.

"We cook a ton," is the way Sarah Blank puts it. The appliances, chosen by her husband, are not just to be looked at. Besides what you'd expect to

Olie and Isaac bed down in the butler's pantry, above. More than a comfy place for the dogs, a steam oven, hidden behind a hopper door, top, makes the pantry a serious cooking center. For the walls Blank chose gum wood that had been salvaged from a tobacco barn.

A sliding cutting board makes the central prep center, left, even more convenient. A carpenter modified a store-bought board so it fits snugly on top of the sink and could easily slide from one side to the other.

BREAD

find in a cook's kitchen this size, there is a high-speed oven in a separate part of the kitchen and a steam oven in the pantry. There are gas ovens for cooking and electric ones for baking.

For Blank, a professional side benefit to all these appliances is when she brings clients into her kitchen to discuss appliance choices and locations, those clients listen.

"Unique" is an over-used word. But it's hard to describe Blank's approach to this design any other way. Planning her kitchen, she realized that features in it would change over time; that it would evolve. Blank couldn't foresee what these changes might be; she could only plan for them.

Two parts of the kitchen show the results of her planning: The area between the island and the refrigerators Blank left open, though it was an ideal spot for more counter space. Much later, she

Kitchen Cabinets are made from butternut wood that was distressed to give it an old New England feel. Old-fashioned latches add to the 19th-century look. Hand-hewn reclaimed ceiling beams are added decorative touches and don't provide structural support for the new additions.

The backsplash, above, is done in 18th-century Delft tiles. Contrary to popular notion, Delft glazes include sepia and white in addition to the more commonly recognized blue and white.

A casual breakfast room takes over the space that had been the original 8- by 11-foot kitchen. The oil cloth rug under the antique table and chairs was painted by Vermont artist Lisa Mair.

found an antique library table. Now it provides extra counter space when needed and its lower height is perfect for baking.

Blank knew one day the wall cabinet next to the refrigerator would be replaced. To prepare for this, she designed a wall that could accommodate a void—an empty spot. This wasn't a critical part of the kitchen, so it was no big deal when the wall cabinet came down. What she found for that spot was a set of stepped shelves. They fit perfectly because Blank had made sure there was sufficient space between the back wall and the window frame so that most antique shelving would fit.

To Your Kitchen

From the Designer

AT THE DESIGN stage be aware that things change over time. What you plan for now could be used for some other purpose later. **IF ANTIQUES** or collectibles will be part of your decor, plan places for them and think about where you'll put items you buy in the future. **TROUGH SINKS** that are ideal for food preparation are excellent for keeping beverages on ice when you entertain.

The prep island, top, is also a breakfast bar. When the Blanks entertain, the bar stools at the island become the best seats in the house.

The trim panel on the refrigerator, top right, has a second door that opens up to reveal a corkboard.

The stepped shelving used to display bowls, right, is over 100 years old. Blank bought it after the kitchen was done and installed it next to a refrigerator in place of two wall cabinets that had originally been there.

Long Island

When cooking and entertaining you need a kitchen equal to your obsession. For David that meant a spacious, efficient kitchen free of excess ornamentation and stocked with professional-style tools always at-hand. It needed to be comfortable, too, and an efficient place for a cook to work in—not easy in a galley kitchen nine feet wide.

Twenty-three feet long with just four small windows, the galley was more like a hallway between the entrance and the rest of the house. "Before the renovation," said David, "no matter where you wanted to go—the deck, the living room, your bedroom, you had to go through the kitchen." Forget about efficient appliance placement or a light and airy feel to the space.

As an architect, David had the design skills to transform small into large and dark into light. He had another advantage, too: his nephew, Jonah Miller, a professional chef—and regular house

The heart of this cook's kitchen is a commercial-style range, positioned for ease of use and to give the cook a view of the outdoor grill and smoker used regularly in meal preparation. The island-mounted prep sink directly opposite the range creates what restaurant chefs call a "stand-and-spin" arrangement—a preferred and efficient use of space when space is limited.

REAR
FRONT
OVEN TEMPERATURE
REAR
FRONT
CHAR-GRILL
OVEN FUNCTION
OVEN TEMPERATURE

VIKING
great cookies
TARTINE
BON APPÉTIT
SILVER PALATE COOKBOOK
The Gourmet Cookbook
joy of cooking
THE NEW BASICS COOKBOOK
MAGNOLIA BAKERY
SOUTHERN COOKING
MORTON'S STEAK BIBLE
CHARLESTON DESSERTS
MARCELLA CUCINA
The Provence Cookbook
PATRICIA WELLS
THE BOATHOUSE

guest—who provided the practical guidance to make the new kitchen a cook's kitchen.

David's plan called for widening the kitchen by six feet, space he found by expanding over part of an outside deck. The widened kitchen meant there was room for a 12- by 3-foot island that Miller had said was a key element if the kitchen was going to be used for serious cooking. The bigger kitchen also meant the door leading to the rest of the house could be moved so traffic flow no longer passed through the work trench. A partition wall closed off the old hallway to create a place for a pantry. With a refrigerator on one wall and a pair of freezer drawers under a counter on the other side, food storage is centralized.

The island divides the kitchen down the middle with work centers on both sides. The cooking center revolves around a commercial-style range. Opposite it, and close at hand, is a prep sink and plenty of counter space. A local ordinance bans garbage disposals so David used a base cabinet on the cook's side of the island for trash bins and a recycling center. A second dishwasher is here too.

The other side of the island is where the primary clean-up center is. Wall cabinets, with translucent sliding doors store dishes and glassware. Two banks of drawers keep silverware and serving pieces. All this storage is close to the

Literally the centerpiece of this new kitchen, the island divides the space down the middle and provides 12 feet of running countertop that can be used from either side. And the long island can easily accommodate up to six stools so it can do double duty as a breakfast bar.

Transom windows above the wall cabinets and small windows in the counter backsplash, right, provide good natural lighting at all times of the day. The effect is like a *trompe l'oeil* in which the cabinets appear to float on glass walls.

Custom-made drawer inserts, below left, increase storage and make drawer organization much easier. The result is a neat and uncluttered kitchen.

An outdoor eating area, below right, is just beyond the back door, only a few steps away from the island work counter, which can be used for plating or for a buffet service on less formal occasions.

Countertop appliances close to the range assist in both food prep and food finishing. The arrangement is based on a restaurant food line, which professional cooks consider the most efficient. Cooking utensils above the range are mounted high enough so the cook needn't worry about open flame if he has to reach for one while preparing a dish.

From the Designer ▶ To Your Kitchen

FROSTED GLASS CABINET DOORS allow kitchen items to be easily seen and give the room a feeling of being larger. **UNDER-CABINET ELECTRICAL STRIPS** mean you can have more countertop appliances and you can move those appliances to wherever they are needed. **BEVERAGE COOLERS** are invaluable. You can never have enough chilled drinks, either for guests at dinner parties or for kids coming through the kitchen on their way outside. **WALL STORAGE** keeps pots and pans in sight and handy for the cook and is a good way to use a space where cabinets cannot be mounted. Hanging pots also eliminates bending to take them out of base cabinets.

big dishwasher so putting things away after a meal is easy. All of the drawers have full-extension sliders. This allows every inch of drawer space to be easily reached.

Two under-counter wine coolers on this side of the kitchen form a beverage center where David can host wine tasting for guests while Jonah cooks. Pots and pans that might normally be stored in the base cabinet space taken up by these coolers are now hung on the wall adjacent to them. Open wall storage also eliminates bending—an important consideration if you use the heavier pots that many cooks prefer.

Electrical outlet strips are mounted under all of the wall cabinets, allowing several countertop appliances to be used simultaneously. Just as important, these small appliances can be moved around and used where needed, which increases functionality and allows for multi-tasking at the various work centers.

Ventilation is especially important with a high-BTU-output, commercial-style range. Here, the hood is mounted higher than normal to clear the window. To ensure proper ventilation, the power of the exhaust fan was increased.

Inspired Amateurs

The Clarks had a problem. Their high-priced kitchen designer had just told them they couldn't take down the wall separating their about-to-be remodeled kitchen and the existing greenhouse. Goodbye natural light; goodbye great lake views. Why? The feng shui would be wrong. Positive kitchen energy would escape out of the greenhouse windows. Goodbye high-priced designer. She wasn't the first.

What the Clarks wanted was a kitchen where both could cook at the same time without getting in each other's way and without fighting over who gets to chop with the chef's knife. The best arrangement they could think of was to work across from each other over a shared island in which food preparation functions were duplicated. Two sinks went in—a big one for her and a smaller trough sink for him. So did two knife and utensil drawers and two receptacles for food waste.

The island is designed so that both husband and wife can work at it—across from each other. Mr. Clark prefers to work seated, so the trough sink is within his easy reach. While doing his prep work he can slide the chopping waste to an in-counter receptacle. Drawers on this side of the island store a duplicate set of knives and other food preparation utensils.

Daylight from the greenhouse makes the open kitchen shine

An architect who had worked on an earlier addition was brought in to deal with technical issues, such as how to disguise a post required for ceiling support. Instead they picked Ken Heise from the Wood Shop of Avon in Minneapolis to design the cabinets and help with the space planning. They got everything they wanted and more.

For the casual greenhouse dining area—used all the time for parties—the Clarks bought a glass table. The light green tinted glass table was the starting point for the translucent green glass backsplash behind the cooktop—an alternative they preferred to a tile backsplash. No grout lines to worry about.

A canvas oilcloth art rug by Minnesota artist Mark Larson adds a strong touch of color. Sitting at the table in the summer Mr. Clark likes to watch the feng shui fly away. The moral here: Stand up for what you want. It's your kitchen. At the end of the day, the designer goes home; you have to stay and live with whatever was done or not done.

From the Designer

▶ To Your Kitchen

IF BOTH OF YOU COOK, think about convenient and duplicate storage areas for knives, utensils, and mixing bowls close to your work areas—and also close to the dishwasher. **TWO DISHWASHERS** are a must if you like to entertain. Make sure at least one of them has adjustable shelves to accommodate large pots. **KEEP WHAT YOU CAN** and make it work in the new design. There is no need to tear out or throw away existing things from the kitchen if they are still serviceable. **YOU ARE THE BOSS.** Remember that if your designer wants something you don't.

Cold water spigots over the cooktop or range are popular 21st-century accessories. They let you fill pots where they are used or add water while cooking. New, shallow cooktops allow utensil drawers to be placed under them. The translucent green backsplash was created by painting the wall a shade of light green and then placing a sheet of clear glass over it. The same glass, but this time sanded, was used for the door fronts on the cabinets flanking the cooktop.

A canvas oilcloth art rug under the glass table, left, adds a bright color accent to a room dominated by shades of green and light brown.

Planning centers are an important element in 21st-century kitchens. Below left, we see a small desk in the greenhouse, placed where it can get plenty of natural light yet not far from the island.

The positioning of the cleanup and prep sinks, below right, reflects the way both cooks like to work—face-to-face on either side of the island. The trough sink, when not used for prep, doubles as a wine bucket at parties.

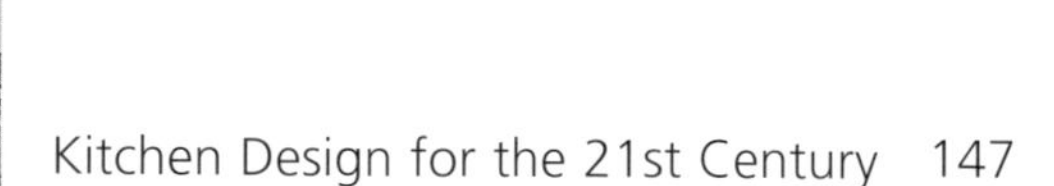

Finders Keepers

This is a kitchen with views. There are outside ones of New York's Hudson River valley and inside ones of the found objects the owners have collected over the years. Not just collectors, these owners are also excellent cooks, which presented Carrie Deane Corcoran of Kitchens by Deane in Stamford, Connecticut with the challenge of designing a kitchen that was a perfect match of efficiency and personality.

Deane Corcoran remembers walking into the old kitchen: It was long and narrow, with not much visible through the windows. Nor was it easy to move around or through it. She also recalls the owners telling her that they wanted to interact with their guests as they prepared meals. But they didn't want guests to see the mess that normally results from cooking a complex meal.

The kitchen's functional center is its long island. In it Deane Corcoran mounted surface cooking units to handle every possible

The 8-foot-long custom range hood provides ventilation for four burners, a wok burner, a deep fryer, and a grill. A high-capacity blower motor provides the exhaust power to vent cooking heat when all those appliances are used simultaneously. The blower is mounted on the roof in order to lessen the fan noise in the kitchen.

cooking task: four standard gas burners, a wok burner, a deep fryer, and a grill. Using any of them, the cook, or both cooks, face into the adjoining room. A raised bar on the island is a convenient place for guests to taste what's being cooked or to just chat with the cooks as they work. It also visually separates the kitchen from the dining room.

Deane Corcoran put two big sinks for cleanup in the counter directly behind all those surface cooking units, creating an efficient galley arrangement similar to a stand-and-spin setup. Two dishwasher drawers to the right of these sinks handle whatever the restaurant high-rise rinser faucet can't. The smaller prep sink she put in the island close to the refrigerator and the pantry. In this location it's accessible from the adjoining room without entering into the work trench.

Now, Deane Corcoran had to find places for all those old objects the owners wanted on display in their new kitchen. The first was a collection of glass jars, actually used for holding staples. Deane Corcoran designed an eight-shelf display unit for them to the left of double built-in ovens. It's handy to the prep sink and the counter area between the sink and the surface cooking units—the kitchen's food preparation center.

The next found object was an old screen door from a bakery, touting its very good bread. The owners bought it years ago and wanted to use it. Deane Corcoran fashioned it as a sliding door to cover the pantry shelves. Well, not exactly. It only

The big island, finished in rustic pine, was designed with a prep sink on the left and a small planning desk on the right. The island's raised back hides the cooking appliances from people in the dining room.

From the Designer

To Your Kitchen

USING FOUND OBJECTS in your kitchen can create surprise; they can bring out your personality. But don't force them into a space. It will lead to something that looks like a mistake. **DON'T BE AFRAID** to take down a wall to get the views you want or to improve traffic flow. **A RAISED BACK** on an island hides cooking appliances, so your guests see you, not the mess.

Good cooks like fast cleanup. That's easy with the commercial, high-rise rinser faucet, top left.

Showing off the owners' personality is an important part of this kitchen's design, which includes open shelving, top right, for their jar collection.

Two steps lead to the lower part of the kitchen, left. Deane Corcoran put a third sink there to handle cooking done on the deck and for potting plants.

covers one side of the pantry shelving; the other side is always open, though it slides back and forth so the owners can decide which side of the pantry they want to close off.

On the other side of the kitchen, opposite this sliding door, is a large 1920s'-era Italian olive oil poster. Making sure there was wall space to hang it was something Deane Corcoran had to consider. Fortunately, the owners didn't need the storage space.

As a warm, inviting backdrop for these found objects, Deane Corcoran selected pine cabinets with a light honey finish. And for island facing, she chose knotty pine boards.

Refrigeration in this kitchen is split between a 36-inch refrigerator/freezer built into a wall and two refrigerator drawers mounted underneath the food prep counter. The drawers keep meats and produce close to where they will be cleaned and cooked. The pantry, with its single, antique sliding door, is in the background.

6

Living Kitchens

In the 21st century, the kitchen will be the center of everything. The rooms around it will be places to eat, play, watch TV, and relax with friends. These rooms will be open and together they will create the 21st century living room.

A Danish Vacation

Open spaces will be the rule in the 21st century; kitchens will merge seamlessly into informal eating areas and comfortable family rooms. There will be a more casual approach to family life, and many people will see their house as a vacation home they live in year-round. Living—good living—will be a key word and the motivation for a more relaxed approach to space planning and design. What we are calling the "living kitchen" will become the centerpiece of a large, open space that will be the true "living room" of the 21st century.

Windy Ridge I, a spec house in suburban Minneapolis, tests these design ideas. The open plan was developer Mark Finholt's vision, executed by architect Todd Hansen and interior designer Dawn Terizzi. Finholt saw his ideal buyer as a well-travelled, well-educated couple with preteen children—a family that would appreciate the "loft living" urban simplicity of Hanson's wide open

The kitchen is the focus of a minimalist open plan combining living, dining, and cooking spaces—three rooms that function as one—where family activities take place casually. The island, also used as breakfast bar, links the kitchen to the rest of the space. Behind the island, open shelves set against tile borrow an idea from contemporary restaurant design.

plan in which it's hard to tell where the kitchen ends and the rest of the space begins.

Finholt and his designers gave this open area a clean, Scandinavian look; they wanted the space to make the design statement, rather than have it made by the stuff in it. Wood plays an important part in this, from the warm Jara floors running throughout to the plain drawer and door style on the fir cabinets. Since wood, even light wood, has the potential to look gloomy in low light, Finholt had Hanson design a monitor window on the roof and extend it over the kitchen and dining rooms. Somewhat like the roof windows in early twentieth-century factories, monitor windows capture sunlight and let it flood into the rooms below. It gives Windy Ridge I a bright, airy feeling all day long, even in overcast weather. It also makes light an important design element for the open plan, which Terizzi took into account in developing her clutter-free interior designs.

There is a family room (just visible through the far doorway in the photo on the previous page), but Finholt chose to orient the kitchen toward the dining and living rooms. These rooms, though modern in style, are intended for the more traditional uses we remember. Sit-down dinners were in the back of everyone's mind as the plans were being drawn. So was casual conversation around the fireplace. Orienting the island so the cook looks in this direction ensures that he or she is involved with the guests at the table or in the living room.

From the Designer

To Your Kitchen

IF THE ISLAND IS PART of the living space, plan it so that it fits with the surrounding design elements. Remember, you'll see the island from other rooms. **MAKE SURE** that rooms within an open space are defined by function so they still feel like separate rooms. Furniture groupings are a good way to do this. **IF YOU LIKE A MINIMAL** style, keep in mind that with a simpler, no-clutter look, any design mistakes will appear more obvious. **HARMONIZE WOOD** colors. Cabinets, trim work, and tables should complement exterior views.

A light monitor, opposite page, lets in natural light all day long. In the evening, low-voltage pendant lights, far left, hung from "hot" cables light the table.

Even in simple, minimalist designs, display space, left, is important, so cabinets on either side of the island have a recessed shelf. This also creates a striking reveal in what otherwise would have been solid wood fronts.

A storage wall of full-height cabinets, below left and right, hides the refrigerator/freezer, a closet, and a walk-in pantry.

The small planning center at the right of the pantry wall, below right, has a place for the phone, a laptop, and the alarm-system monitor.

On the Water

Sunday in the Summer. After church. Time for a casual afternoon supper for 50—prepared in this kitchen. Perhaps not a typical summer pastime. But for these homeowners, active in their church and fortunate enough to have a building lot on Long Island Sound, a kitchen capable of handling the food preparation demands of a large crowd, in a space where everyone could see the water, was the starting point for the design they wanted.

It had to be large and it had to be open. A tough wishlist.

Since the home was new construction, the floor plans and engineering drawings were done by an architect. But figuring how to integrate a working kitchen into the adjacent causual living area—with no partition walls—raised enough questions, so the owners turned to Diane Sawicki, ASID for some help.

Houses built on water often have setback requirements and a maximum allowable lot use. Add to that the natural desire to make

A two-level Island creates an efficient work trench linking the cooking, clean-up and prep centers. The lower counters on both ends of the island are used for serving buffet style and provide extra food prep areas before the luncheon parties begin. The counter seen in the foreground is also a set-down area for baked goods coming out of the wall oven.

Clean **sight lines** enhance the feeling of this **open space**

water views part of the design, and options diminish quickly. Sawicki was aware of this. "When I designed the kitchen I had to adapt to the space, which meant breaking some of the rules of kitchen design."

On paper Sawicki's idea was to establish the core of the kitchen, then build around that core to give the owners what they wanted. She took a novel approach to make this idea easier to execute. After the mechanical systems—plumbing, electrical lines and ductwork—went in, Sawicki photographed the exposed stud walls before other contractors came to hang the drywall. These photos literally gave her a behind-the-scenes look at things and helped her determine the most efficient appliance locations. Just as important, she got the clues she needed to find space that no one else thought was there.

The kitchen core Sawicki designed makes a large, two-tiered island the centerpiece for both food preparation and guest seating. Think of the work counters on this island as a shallow U. The short arms of the U form preparation and set-down surfaces at either end of the kitchen. In the center of this U, Sawicki dropped in a raised breakfast bar with seating for four.

Both of the U's arms have base cabinet storage under the countertops. For the arm closest to the home office, the owners wanted a bank of

A planning center—almost a home office—is tucked under a stairway to the second floor. Now appearing integral to the kitchen space plan, an early design had no place for it. Sawicki's second look, helped by the open stud wall photos she had taken showed her that the under stairway space could be used without affecting other parts of the design.

A compact but efficient work trench, above, puts two sinks within easy reach of the cooks. A third water source is above the range, opposite. Sawicki made good use of the trench's 45-degree corner by placing a TV that is easily seen by guests seated at the island breakfast bar.

drawers. No problem. But they wanted these drawers to match the recessed panel look of the cabinet doors. Sawicki's solution was to have the cabinet maker slice up a door panel and then use the slices as drawer fronts. When assembled and installed, the drawer bank reads like a door, except, of course, for the pulls.

The island's—and the kitchen's—large dimensions convinced Sawicki to double the thickness of the Calcutta marble countertops by installing two slabs. The upper slab was beveled to create an attractive edge design.

To Your Kitchen

From the Designer

LOOK FOR SPACE in unusual places not always obvious on the floorplans. **SLAB MARBLE** cut into tiles allows the backspash to match the counters while offering textural contrast. **WANT A BANK OF DRAWERS** to look like cabinets? Ask your installer to cut a cabinet door into slices that can be used as drawer fronts which, when installed, will reassemble into a panel that matches the cabinet door.

Shelf storage, above, right uses an old-fashioned technique—*glissière de fermature,* "zipper" in English. It's a more secure way to mount heavy glass shelves and offers more adjustment options than are available with shelf pegs.

A banquette along the perimeter of a large bay window, right, lets the casual eating area seat six around a custom-made oval table.

Welcome Warmth

End of the soccer season! This is where team and family members come to celebrate, eat, and relax. There's plenty of room for it: 1200 square feet of open space revolving around a new kitchen, large casual dining room, and a redecorated family room.

It wasn't always that way. The family room, 420 square feet of it, was there, but the old kitchen didn't serve it well and there was no place for a big table. The owners' decision to remodel allowed Moorestown, New Jersey, designer Diane Burgoyne the opportunity to devise a plan that gave the family a bigger, more efficient kitchen; space for the big, sit-down parties they like, and most important, a space plan that unified the family room with areas added by the remodeling. The three open rooms now work together as a single, multi-function living space.

Make it open. That's what the owners wanted. They told Burgoyne to give them enough space so that people could sit at an

Paint and upholstery colors are unifying elements shared by the kitchen and family room. Wall color and architectural detailing similar to the door style of the kitchen cabinets, along with a matching red fabric color used on the kitchen chairs and club chairs around the fireplace, help make these spaces appear as a single, open space.

island while other people sat at a table without feeling cramped. More than that, they insisted that when the chairs were pulled away there would still be 4 feet of clear passage so everyone could move about freely. For Burgoyne, this meant that furniture placement was just as important as appliance placement.

Openness is a function of space. With almost 800 square feet of newly added space under a 10-foot-high ceiling, there was plenty. Calling this a room of grand scale wouldn't be out of place. If anything, Burgoyne had to forget about tricks used by designers to make a small space seem large and figure out ways to scale the room back so it wouldn't overpower the people in it.

The kitchen layout is straightforward; the trench is arranged in an efficient galley. A large, twin-bowl sink in the island serves both prep and cleanup tasks. Behind it is the range. Away from the trench, a larger food preparation center begins to the right of the refrigerator and runs to the wetbar. The family's casual lifestyle and the meals that go with it favor cold food coming out of the 48-inch refrigerator. The long counter is used for both plating and serving this casual fare.

The well-equipped wetbar is where the family likes to use it: right behind the table, which can easily seat ten people, and close to the outdoor patio where casual American barbecue is a regular part of summer living.

Ceiling height contributes to the kitchen's openness. This height also allowed Burgoyne to design a decorative tray ceiling above the island. The molding around it breaks up what could have easily become a monotonous expanse of bland tone. Inside the tray, the red she chose matches the colorway of the fabrics in the family room, which helps to unify the two spaces.

Ideal for both large family gatherings and entertaining friends, the big island, right and opposite page, and the big table beyond it let people sit at both without feeling cramped.

The built-in wall unit, right, has a wide-screen TV that can be seen by people sitting at the island. Next to the TV is an aquarium.

A full-service wetbar with storage for both chilled and unchilled wines, below left, shows an ideal positioning of a work center along the kitchen perimeter. Though some distance from the rest of the kitchen, its location provides all that's needed where it will be used.

> **From the Designer ▶ To Your Kitchen**
>
> **MIXING LIGHT AND DARK** cabinet finishes is routinely done in kitchen design, but in large rooms, contrast helps with balance and scale. **CREATE HARMONY AND UNITY** with color accents that repeat in the spaces that you want to unify. **OVERSIZE FABRIC PATTERNS** on window treatments and upholstered furniture will trick the eye into thinking a space is smaller than it is. **WETBARS** should be placed where they will be used reguarly and where they will take the pressure off the kitchen.

The big table helped Burgoyne deal with room scale because she could place eight oversized chairs around it, just as she put five large stools at the island.

Two other tricks helped scale back the room. The first was running a top course of wall cabinets up to the ceiling and topping them with crown molding. Since these cabinets are hard to reach, many of them are dummy fronts. Those without dummy fronts store seasonal items. Without these extra cabinets and molding, there would be an almost 2-foot gap between the wall cabinet tops and the ceiling. The second trick was choosing a very large fabric pattern for the window treatments—side panels that frame a window wall, which follows the curve of the barrel-vaulted ceiling.

This fabric repeats in the family room where it catches the eye and helps visually link the rooms. But more was needed to unify these rooms. The solution was combining new architectural detailing and strong color accents.

Burgoyne designed a fireplace mantel to cover up what had been bare brick. Above that, more molding to frame a painting and create a visual focal point. The molding's style relates to the door style on the kitchen cabinets; the finish is the same. The two large club chairs with ottomans, upholstered in red, balance the neutral wall tones and move the eye away from the high ceilings—exactly the same effect that the bar stools have at the island.

Totally Open

Barns. When you think of them, what comes to mind first is all that open space and all the things you can do with it. Judith Ann Paixao was thinking this way when she and her late husband bought this Connecticut barn, built in 1880, that had once been owned by George Balanchine.

It needed a major remodeling.

Paixao and her husband, an architect, had two goals. First, was to change the living area around by moving the public spaces—kitchen, living room, and dining room to the upper level. The bedrooms were on that level when they bought the barn. The second goal was building, as Paixao calls it, a house inside of a barn.

The barn's upper level had two haylofts, linked by a 10-foot bridge. It also had a 25-foot-high roof peak and all of the exposed timber framing that make barn architecture so visually appealing. It gave them the space for a totally open living area—an important

Barn red—what else would you expect in a barn—and natural wood are the primary colors here. Wrought iron door pulls and gate hinges on the cabinets add to the barn's nineteenth-century feel. So do the doors on the refrigerator. They are from an old icebox and were bought on the internet. Judith Ann Paixao's carpenter adpated them to fit.

element when a living kitchen merges with the living rooms around it. This is where Paixao built her house. And that house has a distinct eighteenth-century feel. There are old pieces of furniture, some in classic American Federal, others in American Primitive. The interior barn architecture, while not diminished, is in the background, a frame for the decor, the antiques, and the oil paintings on one of the end walls. "You know this is a barn," says Paixao, "but it's the furnishings that strike you first."

The barn's upper-level layout determined the space planning. The kitchen and dining room are in one loft, the living room, across the bridge, in the other. In designing the kitchen, Paixao and her husband didn't want any appliances visible because they didn't want to call attention to the kitchen as something separate from the surrounding open spaces. They were helped here because there were no walls on which to hang cabinets.

At 150 square feet, their kitchen isn't large. They laid it out in a traditional U shape, with a small island that divided the kitchen from the dining room. It's just large enough for four stools so that people can sit across from Paixao when she cooks. And she does a lot of that—for lots of people—so she put a large commercial-style range in the island. Besides four burners, it has a

In a barn everything is open. In fact, barn layouts may be the historical prototype for today's open, living kitchen. In planning the appliance placement in this barn kitchen, Paixao put the range in the island, so that she could talk to guests in the dining rooms and also have a clear view of the fireplace in the living room.

griddle and a grill: more than enough to provide for the twelve to sixteen people who can fit comfortably around the dining room table.

An interesting twist in hiding appliances came about when Paixao considered the best way to hide the refrigerator. An eBay search came up with a set of early twentieth-century icebox doors offered for sale. She bought them and had her carpenter adapt and fit them onto her built-in refrigerator. You have to look twice at them before you realize there's a modern refrigerator behind them.

Barns are the last word in open spaces. Taking advantage of this, Paixao placed the island so she could look across the bridge to the fireplace in the living room. The island's central location also lets her talk with guests at the table or, more likely, when they have sat themselves down on the ladder leading to the barn's crow's nest.

But if barns give you lots of open space to play with, they don't give you a lot of options for kitchen storage. With no wall cabinets possible, the U-shape layout provided the maximum amount of base cabinet storage possible in a kitchen this size. Even so, more was needed. This took the form of a china cabinet, painted in barn red, the predominant color throughout the house. Paixao put the cabinet in the barn's silo, which in the final floorplan ended up next to the dining room. This puts dish, glassware, and linen storage close to the big 12-foot dining table. Also in the silo is a small desk.

From the Designer

▶ To Your Kitchen

IN TOTALLY OPEN SPACE, plan your kitchen so it relates to everything around it. **BASE CABINETS** are a more practical way to store things than wall cabinets, and you won't have to reach for items stored on high selves. **DON'T LIKE** the options that cabinet manufacturers give you to hide appliances? Alternatives are available. A good carpenter will be able to adapt whatever you buy so it fits on the appliance you want to hide.

The simple barn kitchen, left, is only 150 square feet. No walls meant no wall cabinets, which was fine with the owners, who wanted their kitchen to be indistinguishable from the surrounding rooms.

Family portraits hang on the dining room wall, opposite page. The table, with large chairs upholstered in red to match the barn's primary color, is large enough to seat sixteen people comfortably. The stairs in the background lead to the lower level.

Old bottles and jars, below left, are on display on a ledge where the roof meets the wall.

Ocean Breezes

Soft translucent blue, the color of the ocean on a clear day—this is the color of this kitchen every day. This is a summer house on the New Jersey shore—the beachfront if you don't know the Jersey slang for living on the ocean. When you live on the shore with the Atlantic as your neighbor, there is an irresistible urge to include the ocean in the way you live.

That's what happened here, brought to life in a collaboration between Michelle Slemmer, CKD, of Apple Kitchens and Diane Burgoyne of Diane Burgoyne Interiors—both Moorestown, New Jersey, firms. Besides ocean influences, the plan they came up with owes its inspiration to the curved stainless-steel railings that define all of the spaces in this house.

These curves motivated Slemmer to design an island shaped like a question mark, its convex end mating perfectly with the concave area across from it where the dining table sits. Other

A simple space plan, with the cleanup sink on the island and the prep sink in the corner between the refrigerator and the cooktop, is set up for cooking the lighter fare that's part of summertime living by the ocean. Ocean colors, translucent blues and greens, link the kitchen and casual living spaces with the long views of the sea visible out every window.

An open plan lets the kitchen and adjoining rooms enjoy great views of the ocean

The entertainment center, left, built into a wall unit of light wood, adds warmth to a color scheme inspired by the pale blues and greens of the ocean.

The space plan, based on the curved forms of the room railings, determined that convex and concave forms had to fit together visually like pieces of a puzzle—the inward sweep of the island suggesting a home for the round dining table. Above the island the monorail lighting repeats the island's question-mark form.

aspects of her plan are more straightforward: 230 square feet of space, a cleanup center in the island, the cooktop opposite it in a stand-and-spin arrangement, a prep sink in the corner. Outside of the trench a single refrigerator/freezer is at one end of an L-shaped counter, a built-in espresso machine at the other.

Putting the plan into practice was less straightforward. During construction, a big structural beam had to be added to support the clear-span ceiling. This required Slemmer to move the coffee station from the corner of the L to the end of the counter. The beam dropped too low to mount the espresso machine. A positive result from this was the addition of the corner prep sink and two windows to provide light for it.

The cabinets are maple that has been painted white. All of them are trimmed in stainless steel: box moldings for the tops of wall cabinets and toe kicks for the base cabinets. Six stainless posts support the boomerang-shaped glass breakfast bar that seems to float above the island.

With the kitchen planned, Burgoyne began to work out the color scheme and to design furniture to complement the open, curvilinear space. To create the shimmering effect of the ocean, she found one-inch-square translucent green tiles; she mounted these on the backsplashes. Playing off them are blue Swarovski crystal pendant lights dropping from a monorail above the island. Continuing the blue and green theme, she used a solid, pale green fabric for the bar stools and dining room chairs. In the living room a blue and green patterned upholstery fabric on the sectional sofa and chairs harmonizes with the kitchen colors.

From the Designer ▶ To Your Kitchen

KEEP YOUR COLOR PALETTE simple when coordinating indoor and outdoor colors. **USE WOOD AND FURNITURE** to add warmth to contemporary spaces and to make them appear less stark. **POSITION YOUR** work centers so you can take advantage of the great views through your windows.

This kitchen is a study in curved forms and stainless steel. The faucet, above left, with its bowling-pin–like base and bending spout, repeats the island's question-mark shape.

Stainless steel bar stools, above right, have curved back supports that sweep down into footrests. Their pale green upholstered seats play into the color scheme established by the backsplash tiles.

The Art Deco range hood, left, ruled out putting wall cabinets close to the cooktop. To make up for this there are two deep pot drawers under it. These are flanked by pull-out pantry units to store items normally kept up above.

The coffee station, left, was fit into a modified pantry cabinet rotated 90 degrees—necessitated by window placement.

Pendant lights, above, dropping from a monorail, provide both task and ambient lighting. When on, the blue Swarovski crystals throw a cool, ocean-quality light across the room.

Burgoyne saw the furniture as decorative detailing that would warm up the open, contemporary space. The Brazilian cherry floor that forms a backdrop to the shore colors—white, blue, and green—was conceived as a furniture-like element. She had to convince the owners that the darker floor created a better balance in the room than the lighter one they originally wanted, however.

The dining table, the bookcase built into the back of the sofa, and the entertainment unit add more contrast and balance established by the warm cherry floor. But the most interesting furniture elements are the dining chairs. They are classically styled Greek Revival side chairs, but rather than making them of wood, Burgoyne had them fabricated in stainless steel to fit in with the other stainless details in the space.

The People behind the Projects

Abruzzo Kitchens; pgs. 28, 30
Maureen O'Neill
1105 Remington Road, Suite E
Schaumburg, IL 60173
847-885-0500
www.abruzzokitchens.com

Apple Kitchens; pg. 22
513 Lenola Road
Moorestown, NJ 08057
856-235-2295
applekitchens@verizon.net

Brooks & Falotico Associates; pgs. 30, 32-33, 38
199 Elm Street
New Canaan, CT 06840
203-966-8440
www.brooksandfalotico.com

Bzak Design Group; pgs. 26, 38
614 Wooster Pike
Terrace Park, OH 45174
513-831-3155
www.bzakdesigngroup.com

Crystal Cabinetry; pg. 38-39
www.crystalcabinets.com

Dacor; pg. 32
www.dacor.com

Diane Burgoyne Interiors; pgs. 27, 39
1223 N. Church Street
Moorestown, NJ 08057
856-234-9660
www.dianeburgoyneinteriors.com

Diana Sawicki Interior Design; pgs. 19, 38-39,
Diana Sawicki, ASID
46 Riverside Avenue
Westport, CT 06880
203-454-5890
dianasawicki@aol.com

Dorado Designs; pgs. 14, 26
4640 E. Sunrise Drive, Suite 118
Tucson, AZ 85718
520-577-1800
www.doradodesigns.com

Ecostone by Constantion; pg. 41
www.silesone.com

Forbo Flooring pg. 39
www.forbo-flooring.com

Kirei Bamboo; pg. 41
www.kireiusa.com

Liebherr; pg. 33
www.liebherr-appliances.com

Huestis Tucker Architects; pgs. 2-3, 35
2349 Whitney Avenue
Hamden, CT 06518
203-248-1007
www.huestistuckerarchitects.com

Julianne Stirling Design Associates; pgs. 30
Julianne Stirling, ASID
info@stirlingdesignassociates.com

Kitchens by Deane; pgs 4, 15, 25, 32, 34, 39
1267 East Main Street
Stamford, CT 06902
203-327-7008
www.kitchensbydeane.com

Kitchen Design Studio of New Canaan; pgs. 9, 33
www.kitchendesignstudio.com

Kohler Company; pg. 33
www.kohlerco.com

Living Spaces Inc; pgs. 24, 31
2678 Orchard Lake Road
Sylvan Lake, MI 48320
248-682-3600

Mark P Finlay Architects, AIA; pg. 10
96 Old Post Road, Suite 200
South Port, CT 06890
203-254-2388
mpfaia@markfinlay.com

North Star Kitchens; pgs. 12-13
275 Market Street, Suite 162
Minneapolis. MN 55405
612-375-9533
www.northstarkitchens.com

Perlick; pg. 33
www.perlick.com

Plain and Fancy; pg. 29
www.plainfancycabinetry.com

Steven & Associates; pg. 16
Steven Ptaszek, CKD
612-573-0321
ckdesigner@yahoo.com

Teragren; pg. 40
www.perlick.com

Toni Gallagher Interior Design; pgs. 11, 20
914-967-3594
toniginteriors@aol.com

Troy Adams; pg. 32
www.troyadamsdesign.com

Tsao Designs; pgs. 6-7
Mai and Warren Arthur
203-335-4337

Chapter 3

Raising Arizona, pg. 45
Kameron Rutschman
Dorado Designs
4640 E. Sunrise Drive, Suites 118
Tucson, AZ 85718
520-577-1800
www.doradodesigns.com

Life On An Island, pg. 52
Louise Brooks, AIA
Brooks & Falotico Associates
199 Elm Street
New Canaan, CT 06840
203-966-8440
www.brooksandfalotico.com

Stylist: Carolyn J Shultz

Eyes for the Past, pg. 58
Christine Donner
Christine Donner Kitchen Design Inc.
New Canaan, CT 06840
203-966-0160
www.donnerkitchens.com

Blue And White pg. 64
Toni Gallagher Interior Design
914-967-3594
toniginteriors@aol.com

Stylist: Tina Armstrong
Tina Armstrong Interiors
212-570-1981

Bay Area Beckons, pg. 72
Mark E Kendall
Kenmark Construction
360 Post Street
San Francisco, CA 94108
415-782-5500
mkendall@kenmark.com

Arsenio Perez Jr., CKD
KB Associates
14 E. 25th Avenue
San Mateo, CA 94403
707-425-2869
kbap@onemain.com

Chapter 4

Entertain Anytime, pg. 81
Judy Larson
Judith Larson Associates
4 Forest Street
New Canaan, CT 96840
203-972-1409
jladesigns@aol.com

Bill Gardiner
www.gardinerlarson.com

Stylist: Kyle L. Riccoboni
Creative Director, Earth Garden
Wilton, CT

Friendly Formality, pg. 88

Mary Jo Peterson, CKD
203-775-4763
www.mjpdesign.com

Sam Cousins
Hemingway Custom Cabinetry, LLC
3400 Fairfield Avenue
Black Rock, CT 06605
203-382-0300
scousins@charter.net

European Vision, pg. 94

Julia Zemp
New Canaan Kitchens
19 South Avenue
New Canan, CT 06840
203-972-8300
www.newcanaankitchens.com

Frederick C. Allen
Fine Homebuilders Inc.
203-221-8153
finehomebuilder@aol.com

In Good Company, pg. 103

Ellen Bailey Dickson, AIA
Bailey Edward Design
900 North Franklin, Suite 604
Chicago, IL 60610
312-440-2300
www.bedesign.com

Moveable Feast, pg. 110

Allen Shope AIA
Listening Rock Farm
845-877-6335
apshope@gmail.com

Eric Furno
Furno Architects
14 E. 25th Avenue
203-637-8138
efurno@furnoarchitects.com

Shaw Builders
New Preston, CT
860-868-1040
www.shawbuilder.com

Stylist: Carolyn J Shultz

Chapter 5

Kitchen On Line, pg. 121

Rand O'Kane, CKD
Bilotta Kitchens
1564 Mamaroneck Avneue
Marmoneck, NY 10543
914-381-7734
www.bilotta.com

Maurices Olde World Furnishings
950 Jupiter Park Drive
Jupiter, FL 33458
561-747-4339
www.mauricepine.com
Thomas A. Conway, AIA
The Rosen Group
16 Maple Street
Summit, NJ 07901
908-273-6565
www.rosengroup.net

Stylist: Carolyn J Shultz

American Nostalgia, pg. 129

Sarah Blank, CKD
SBD Kitchens LLC
1472 Post Road.
Darien, CT
203-972-8341
www.sbdkitchens.com

Lisa Mair
lisa@canvasworks.com

Stylist: Sarah Shaw
Shaw_srh@yahoo.com

Long Island, pg. 134

David M. Swartz Architects
www.dmsas.com

Stylist: Carolyn J Shultz

Inspired Amateurs, pg. 143

Ken Heise
The Woodshop of Avon
3918 Sunnyside Road
Edina, MN 55424
952-927-8002
www.thewoodshopofavon.com

Finders Keepers, pg. 149

Carrie Deane Corcoran
Kitchens by Deane
89 Elm Street
New Canaan CT 06840
203-972-8836
www.kitchensbydeane.com

Chapter 6

A Danish Vacation, pg. 157

Mark Finholt
Birch River
16470 Kingswood Drive
Lakeville, MN 55044
952-435-8127
www.birchriver.com

Todd P. Hanson, AIA
Albertsson Hansen Architecture, Ltd.
1005 West Franklin Avenue
Minneapolis, MN 55405
612-823-0233
www.aharchitecture.com

Dawn Terizzi, Casa Bella Designs
763-552-0073

Finn Style
612-341-4075
www.finnstyle.com

Design Within Reach
In Minneapolis, 612-827-0990
800-944-2233
www.dwr.com

Rich Rosenberg, Inc.
612-333-4673

Aubrey-Angelo
www.aubry-angelo.com

On The Water, pg. 160

Diane Sawicki, ASID
Diana Sawicki Interior Design
46 Riverside Avenue
Westport, CT 06880
203-454-5890
dianasawicki@aol.com

Stylist: Carolyn J Schultz

Welcome Warmth, pg. 169

Diane Burgoyne
Diane Burgoyne Interiors
1223 N. Church Street
Moorestown, NJ 08057
856-234-9660
www.dianeburgoyneinteriors.com

Totally Open, pg. 174

Judith Ann Paixao
annpaixio@aol.com

Ocean Breezes, pg. 181

Michelle Slemmer, CKD
Apple Kitchens
513 Lenola Road
Moorestown, NJ 08057
856-235-2295
applekitchens@verizon.net

Diane Burgoyne
Diane Burgoyne Interiors
1223 N. Church Street
Moorestown, NJ 08057
856-234-9660
www.dianeburgoyneinteriors.com

Connecticut Photographics
Mark Savoia & Cathy Vanaria
1-800-CT-PHOTO
www.ctphoto.com

Cabinetry by Wood-Mode, Inc
To find a showroom visit
www.wood-mode.com

INDEX